The New
English Class

Karen —

Thank for the

support!

B

The New English Class:

A GUIDE TO THE WRITING GAME LINGUA GALAXIAE

Bryan Steele

Interior graphics design: John Beach Design, Los Angeles CA

ISBN: 978-0-9705070-3-7

Library of Congress Control Number: 2015919695

Foreshadow Press: Longmont, Colorado

www.Foreshadow.Press

Table of Contents

About the Author

Bryan Steele served meritoriously in the US Marine Corps followed by eight years trading for commercial banking clients on and off the floor of the Chicago Mercantile Exchange. Steele then left the securities industry and attended UC, Irvine, to study English under such luminaries as Jacques Derrida. Afterwards, Steele attended graduate school while he taught inner city high school English in Los Angeles. After five years of teaching, Steele moved to the *LA Weekly* where he exposed administrative dysfunction within the Los Angeles school district. As a result of his work for the *Weekly*, Steele was hired by the California Legislature where, armed with subpoena power, he investigated public-school issues statewide, held public hearings, and issued legislative reports – five of which are held by the US Library of Congress. Steele's many publishing credits include *Road to Belmont*, in which he documents the causal relationship between adult administration and student success.

Foreword

This book is not an attempt to replicate the writing game, Lingua Galaxiae, which teaches process through practice. So, keep in mind while reading that the central value of the Game comes from the guided practice of process, the daily writing and critiquing, not from the kind of general understanding this book provides.

What this book does attempt to do is to provide theoretical background for each of the Game's 88-steps. If you are looking for a better understanding of the Game than is provided here, or if you believe some aspect of the book or Game is deficient, then academically assert yourself and play the Game. Lingua Galaxiae is not a thing; it is a system for managing change.

**A video tour of the Game, Lingua Galaxiae, is available for viewing here: http://linguagalaxiae.com/tour.html
Viewing this video is essential for understanding this book.
Please view this video now or when it is referenced later in Chapter 1.**

CHAPTER 1

Learning and Gaming

> Language is the only instrument of science,
> and words are but the signs of ideas.
> SAMUEL JOHNSON,
> PREFACE TO *ENGLISH DICTIONARY*

High-school English is significantly deficient on two fronts: we are failing to teach students the nature of language while simultaneously failing to teach epistemology, that is, how we know what we know. A solution to these deficiencies is Lingua Galaxiae, an intensive online writing game that studies language as a system in the context of change. Each player has a personal writing coach who provides critiques of the player's daily writing assignments and final portfolio and ensures that it is ready for college applications.

Since the advent of modernism, great strides have been made in the areas of language and knowledge. Unfortunately, few of these advancements have made their way into US high-school classrooms. Instead, we have four years of language arts when what we need is a balance of art and science.

The deficiencies in high-school English are glaring when compared to high-school science. There was an explosion of new ideas at the beginning of the twentieth century so that virtually every academic discipline underwent a major transformation, and the science of physics was no exception. A review of high-school physics standards demonstrates the legacy of these early twentieth-century transformations. Although there is no agreed-upon national-science standard as of yet, the following people and ideas appear either directly or indirectly in secondary-science curricula throughout the nation:

1

- **Max Planck** (1858–1947) is the father of quantum theory and the author of Planck's constant.
- **Erwin Schrödinger** (1887–1961) developed a number of insights into the field of quantum theory, which formed the basis of wave mechanics, including his Schrödinger equation and his famous thought experiment, Schrödinger's cat.
- **Louis de Broglie** (1892–1987) also made significant contributions to the world of quantum physics by demonstrating that not only light but all matter functions as either a wave or a particle.
- **Werner Heisenberg** (1901–1976) was another important contributor to the world of quantum physics and is best known for his uncertainty principal.

Although there was a similar explosion of new ideas pertaining to language around the beginning of the twentieth century, the English Common Core makes no mention of these people, their ideas, or any of the academic developments since then—as if the twentieth century never happened. Putting aside the Common Core's failure to mention the Greeks, Thomas Aquinas, or John Locke in the context of language, the Common Core makes no mention of those who helped shape the modern era of language theory and epistemology, such as the following:

- Friedrich Nietzsche
- Ferdinand de Saussure
- Roman Jakobson
- Sigmund Freud
- Karl Popper
- Roland Barthes
- Jacques Derrida

There is not a single mention of any of their contributions to the modern understanding of language anywhere in the Common Core. It is not hyperbole to conclude that today's Common Core English standards would feel as much at home in a classroom 150-years ago as they do today. The end result is a population made less aware about the very tool necessary for thinking: language.

Any claim that language theory is too complicated or controversial for the high-school classroom is utter nonsense. I challenge anyone to identify any portion of present-day language theory that comes even close to the intellectual demands and controversy generated by the inexplicable but observable reality of quantum mechanics where an atom can be observed in either of 2 contradictory situations (Rosenblum).

A great deal can be said as to why high-school science has kept up with the advancements in research while high-school English has not. However, that is not the point of this book or the Game, Lingua Galaxiae. Rather, this approach to language study is concerned with taking stock of where we are now and moving forward by providing an understanding of language and epistemology that is accessible to the average sixteen-year-old.

The Game and Language Theory

Why is teaching language theory so important? Because it is through the discipline of language theory that language can be discussed successfully as a whole system of interacting parts. The *wholeness* of language as a system, the listing of the many parts of language, is supplied by all the accomplishments of those theorists, beginning with the ancient Greeks, who helped develop what is today a complex understanding of language (chapter 8).

Beyond the merely rational, to understand language is to free the mind to wonder. Consider the impact of Albert Einstein's theory of general relativity not just on physics and the other sciences, but also on the larger public imagination. While Einstein was challenging Newton's laws, literature and poetry were being revolutionized respectively by James Joyce and T. S. Eliot. At the same time, Pablo Picasso was busy changing the nature of line and perspective while Henri Matisse was changing the way we think about color. In music, tonality was forever being changed by Igor Stravinsky and Arnold Schoenberg.

The world of wonderment brought on by the likes of Einstein, Planck, and Heisenberg provided physics with thought experiments that are still used today to push the envelope of physics by suggesting further areas of research. If wonderment fosters a greater understanding of physics, then why can't wonderment do the same for language? By failing to teach the nature of language in high school, we are foregoing all of the unknown advances that could come from a better understanding of the very tool we use to think and communicate.

Then there is the practical side of things. Teaching the nature of language is also important because it enhances problem-solving skills. As will be discussed in chapter 4, the first step of analyzing a system is to discover all its parts; this also happens to be the first step of problem solving: understanding the context of a problem by discovering all of the influences relating to some dysfunctional outcome.

Additionally, teaching the nature of language protects the individual and the group from those who covertly manipulate language for profit and power. The discussion of systems theory in chapter 5 explains why the manipulation of language undermines the ability of human systems to achieve purposefully set goals, and the discussion of propaganda in chapter 10 explains how this undermining of language is accomplished.

The political ramifications of teaching language as a system can be found in the contrast between Plato's concern for "Who should rule?" and Karl Popper's question of "How do we arrange our institutions to prevent rulers (whether individuals or majorities) from doing too much damage?" While Plato is concerned with the politics of who is elected, Popper is concerned about the corrupting influence of human nature regardless of who is elected.

Learning about the nature of language in the context of systems theory provides more information along with the tools for managing this increased volume of information, which results in increased overall awareness—not to mention better grades and a greater sense of self.

The Game and Systems Theory

A common theme throughout the modern era was the replacement of the simple with the complex. In every example of modern thinkers, the respective disciplines were expanded or created to be understood, not as a grouping of individual and autonomous parts but as systems of interacting parts. The modern era is full of such examples, including the parallel development of atomic and language theories.

At the beginning of the twentieth century, the smallest unit of matter was the individual atom; likewise, the smallest unit of language was the individual word. Both disciplines underwent a fundamental change as atoms became understood not as autonomous individual *things* but as systems of interacting parts. In the same way, modernism ushered in an era in which words themselves were no longer considered individual things but were now understood as systems of interacting parts (chapter 8).

In both linguistics and physics, the classical notion of *difference* gave way to the more sophisticated interactions of systems. Chapter 8 explains the role *difference* plays in meaning and the way in which, upon closer inspection, differences of meaning are interconnected through a *relationship* of opposing parts that make up a whole.

If *A* cannot exist without *B*, when *A* and *B* represent a relationship between two sides of the same coin, then how do you separate *A* from *B* for the purpose of defining their difference?

The same concept is alive in physics, where the parts of an atom are understood not to be autonomous but to exist as the result of relationships. A similar analogy can be found in the elements of time, space, and matter, all existing as a relationship of parts. Writing in 2015 for *Scientific American Magazine*'s issue celebrating one hundred years of general relativity, Walter Isaacson explains,

> With his special theory of relativity, Einstein had shown that space and time did not have independent existence but instead formed a fabric of space-time. Now, with his general version of the theory, this fabric of space-time became not merely a container for objects and events. Instead, it had its own dynamics that were determined by, and in turn helped to determine, the motion of objects within it.

The Game concludes by drawing on the theme of the relationship between differences by juxtaposing propaganda with the nature of language. Rather than a distinct set of ideas, propaganda is understood as the mirror opposite of the rules governing language as defined by the Game. From the perspective of propaganda, the game's Rules of Discovery and Logic are not defining parameters that limit and guide language use as it relates to the physical world but are a proactive part of the propagandist's tool box for manipulating language in service to the agendas of those who pay.

Similar expansions of understanding during the modern era that applied a systems approach include the following:

- Sigmund Freud expanding the understanding of the human psyche to include a system of three interacting parts: the Id, the Ego, and the Super Ego;
- Karl Marx, pushing back against the self-serving economic models of his day, insisted that economics be understood as a whole system that must include all of its relevant parts, including labor;
- Ferdinand de Saussure explaining how words (signs) are not isolated units but are comprised of interacting parts, the *signifier* and the *signified*, that interact like two sides of the same coin.

Despite the complexity of all of these systems, the most complex of all systems is the system that accounts for our internal selves. This complex system of self-knowledge is also directly tied to learning (chapter 3). As such, the Game begins with the question "Who am I?" Incorporating quotes from virtually every major thinker throughout world history, the Game requires each player to ask "Who am I?" throughout the game. Furthermore, the Game makes this question an integral part of the Game's final portfolio assessment.

The application of systems theory to language is particularly significant for the Game because of the role played by the individual. The Game's primary structure of language is the interplay among three forces:

- Linguistic **Operation** of language
- Human nature of the **Operator** of language
- **Rules** mitigating the relationship between the *Operator* and *Operation* of language

The Game presents these three competing ideas as its primary learning structure, which is represented by a triangle of competing forces where each element stands in a collective relationship of tension and balance with the other two. Human nature is an essential part of language because language does not meaningfully exist outside of its use. As such, it is not possible to separate the human mind from its use of language.

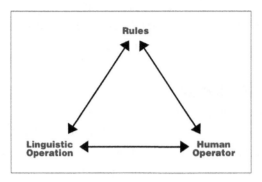

Language as a system of interacting parts

As will be discussed in chapter 5, systems theory demands attributes that keep the human *Operator* in check. These attributes include the following:

- Wholeness
- Accountability
- Transparency
- Integrity
- Balance
- Sustainability

It is through the demands of systems theory that human tendencies to cut corners in the pursuit of self-interest is kept at bay in service to the system's purposeful goals. Systems theory does not make these demands because of some moral code but because of self-interest built from heightened awareness of the greater whole. By incorporating these ideas into the Game, the player learns through the practice of *process* rather than the memorization of *content*.

The modern era ushered in an awakening to the idea that understanding was not a product of *difference* but a product of a far more complex set of relationships forever in a state of change. It is systems theory that provides us with the tools to comprehend and manage this new world of constantly changing and complex relationships. Through the work of famed Austrian biologist Ludwig von Bertalanffy and his book *General System Theory*, the Game focuses on the introduction and formal development of systems theory in the twentieth century to build its framework (chapter 5). But before this can happen, the Game introduces an idea that is as relevant today as it was when the ancient Greeks began struggling with it two and a half millennia ago: change.

The Game and Change

Chapter 2 discusses how the Game addresses change, but, for now, it is important to understand how the Game itself practices what it preaches. How do you teach and test for an idea that is defined as a moving target? But, more fundamentally, how do you teach change when the answer itself might conceivably change between now and Friday's test? The answer is to teach *process* over *content* so that the lesson is not the memorization of individual academic units but the practice of processes. This notion of content versus process is essential to understanding the Game in that *process* is the management of *content*. Lingua Galaxiae teaches elements of content, but only secondarily, as the primary focus is on process.

Augmenting this structure of championing process over content is the characterization of all the Game's ideas as "tools." These tools are like those found around the house, in that they require the following:

- Training
- Skill building
- Maintenance
- Replacement

In this way, the ideas, or tools, of the Game accommodate change. The first tool of the Game is the question "Who am I?" This question is a perfect example of a tool because of the way it represents *process* over *content*. You have to be honest with teens and acknowledge that the question of self-knowledge can never be fully known, no matter how much effort an individual puts into the investigation. Therefore, the question of self-knowledge is not a *thing*, or an element of *content*, but a *process*. And because change is constant, the process of asking the question, the tool itself, will evolve as the individual evolves.

The notion of *wholeness* provides another good example of a Game tool. Systems theory requires that practitioners seek to account for all elements of a system so as to understand the whole system. But, of course, it is not possible to know whether all parts have been accounted for because that would require omnipotent knowledge of all places and times. Therefore, the tool of *wholeness* is not a thing but a process for making a best effort at accounting for all the parts of a system.

The Game's rules and definitions are themselves tools, as is evidenced by the first rule: "The physical world is in a constant state of change." This emphatic statement is intended to challenge the player. All a player needs in order to challenge this statement is to find a single contradictory example. As players rack their brains, trying to think of a way to prove this statement wrong, they are learning process. When players think an example justifying change has been found and attempt to apply the example, they are learning process. When players think they have succeeded but are then shown the error of their analysis, they are learning process.

If you have not yet watched the video tour of the game, please do so now: http://linguagalaxiae.com/tour.html

Further complicating the discussion of change is the question of how to teach process when even process itself is susceptible to change. The Game satisfies this quandary not only by accommodating change, but also by proactively encouraging players to change the Game for points. Players use the Game's own rules and definitions, along with outside evidence, to demonstrate examples of inconsistency within the Game. Putting students in a position of academic authority is potentially problematic as lessons could become untethered from their academic foundations and drift off into meaninglessness. The answer is facilitated by the Game *via* the requirement that any effort to gain points through a game change (Change Order) be accomplished through a demanding academic process. To attempt changing the Game, a player must present a

Change Order to the Gamemaster that satisfies the following criteria within a set minimum and maximum word count:

1. **Identify**. Where should the game be changed?
2. **Solve**. How should the game be changed?
3. **Argue**. Why should the game be changed?
4. **Support**. Provide evidence to support your change.
5. **Conclude**. Advocate for your Change Order in a single sentence of fewer than twenty-one words or, for extra points, compose your conclusion as a haiku.

Change Orders are submitted to the Gamemaster, who either rejects it or initiates a back and forth exchange of edits until the Change Order is accepted. If it is accepted, the player receives points. If the Change Order involves either a glossary definition or code rule, the respective definition or rule is changed and the content of the Change Order is permanently recorded as historical precedent through a pop-up icon attached to the respective definition or rule. In this way, not only can the game be changed by a player, the history of any change is recorded and made available, just as precedent functions within the law.

This back and forth exchange of text between player and Gamemaster effectively provides players with a private writing coach throughout the Game's four-month cycle. Due to the fact that the Gamemaster is required to edit player essays within twenty-four hours of submission, there is a cap on the number of players each Gamemaster can accommodate. For each essay, the Gamemaster provides comments using colored text within the player's text, as well as comments in a separate field, all of which stays with the player's respective essay throughout the Game.

This is how to teach writing: practice, practice, and more practice with a tutor looking over the student's shoulder and providing advice. Lingua Galaxiae provides each player with a level of writing instruction that is even better than a private tutor because the roles of writing coach and Step production are kept separate; this allows for a team of educators to focus on different specific tasks. The Game combines the efforts of these two elements to create a product that would be impossible for a single person to produce. In short, Lingua Galaxiae represents a model of education that could only be replicated by an institution through significant increases in the number of and assignment of teaching staff.

In each player's private domain is the My Points page that breaks down the player's points into five categories:

- Change Orders (accepted)
- List Change (add/delete from a list, add/delete a list)
- Player Recruitment (player's friend/associate completes sign up)
- Step Completion (Step essay is returned from Gamemaster, revised, and saved)
- General (miscellaneous content, including ways to earn extra points listed on the Player Commons page)

The Game proactively manages exchanges between the player and Gamemaster internally behind the scenes. Whether it involves a submission of a Change Order or a daily Step Essay, the item's pop-up window provides the player with a linear progress chart showing the status of each submission from conception to acceptance. The Game is "smart" in the sense that a player's submission may not move forward until the requirements of a specific step have been satisfied. In this way, players are prevented from building on past mistakes and having to redo previous work, which undermines student motivation.

The encouragement of players to change the Game is an intentional act of tapping into youthful angst. There is no greater motivator of teen learning than explaining how adult ideas are possibly wrong, incomplete, or hypocritical. As teens are transitioning from a life where they have been told what is true, many, by age sixteen, are starting to notice examples of adult hypocrisy. The Game harnesses this burgeoning awareness as a means of stimulating intellectual curiosity and action.

The Game and Science Fiction

Why is the Game named Lingua Galaxiae, which is Latin for language of the galaxy? The Game uses a science-fiction backstory that revolves around the future discovery of time travel here on Earth. We are in the twenty-first century, but we still teach language as if Isaac Newton remained the dominant force for understanding the physical world. How can we expect to discover time travel using an archaic understanding of language, which is the primary tool of discovery?

As an antidote, the Game was created and recently seeded on Earth by a group of time travelers with a name that loosely translates as the Coalition of Time Traveling Societies (CUTTS). As the story goes, a newbie time-traveling civilization disrupted one of CUTTS' annual dinners, and the whole event was ruined; it appears the group arrived late, mined precious metals during the opening ceremony, and then ran off with the emperor's daughter to parts unknown. In the wake of this dreadful affair, CUTTS organized the game Lingua Galaxiae for civilizations about to discover time travel so as to prevent future difficulties. More detail about CUTTS can be found at Facebook.com/CUTTS2040.

Anything with UFOs is great for the classroom. As with most controversies over religion or politics, teachers risk the ire of parents and hurt feelings of students who might be ridiculed for expressing their beliefs. The exception is UFOs, which can generate broad disagreement among students without any blowback; and, besides, UFOs are fun. A great book for reading aloud in the classroom is John Mack's *Abductions*. Mack was a Harvard professor, psychiatrist, and Pulitzer Prize recipient who was disowned by academia for his research on alien abductees.

There is so much information about UFOs available to students. While much of it is junk, a great deal of it is tantalizingly difficult to ignore. For instance, there is former NASA astronaut and Princeton physics professor Brian O'Leary, who has made numerous statements—many available on YouTube—concerning his belief in alien encounters on Earth. Speaking on video shortly before his death in 2011, O'Leary said, "There is abundant evidence that we are being contacted, that civilizations have been visiting us for a very long time". All of this is excellent fodder for discussing the nature of evidence (chapter 4).

The more serious edge of the Game's science-fiction tale is the link between scientific advancement and a more sophisticated understanding of language. Lingua Galaxiae seeks to live up to its name by creating an understanding of language that will speed the discovery of time travel. The study of space-time is vibrant and productive for stimulating thought. Every week sees a handful of new press reports of hard-science news concerning advancements in the understanding of time and space. These reports draw people's attention to scientific journals that usually elude the general public. Yes, the science-fiction story of Lingua Galaxiae is all made up, but the context of the story, current advancements in science, makes for a fun and thrilling tale.

The Game's Player Commons page features a countdown clock that displays the time between now and the discovery of time travel here on Earth, in about twenty-five years, so that a player today could easily be on the future science team that discovers how to conquer time and space. Another section of the Player Commons page, Time Travel in the News, includes hyperlinks to news stories discussing the latest in time-travel-related discoveries. The reason the Game incorporates a science-fiction component is because learning should be fun. Furthermore, identifying an otherwise-unknown third party, CUTTS, as the game's originator eliminates the distraction of teacher adulation; after all, I'm nobody, just the hired help.

The Game and Education Theory

The notion of *wholeness* as described by systems theory goes to the heart of what is known about learning theory: namely, the building of context. Learning is directly tied to context because it is through context that the human brain creates memory—the greater the context, the greater the quality and quantity of the learning experience.

To put it simply, a well-crafted lesson begins with what the student already understands, point A, and then moves in small digestible steps to the lesson objective, point B, without ever letting the student feel adrift. By formally incorporating the tool of wholeness into the classroom, the instructor strives to maximize context.

Another reason that context is tied to learning is because humans learn in different ways. Context provides greater complexity and, thereby, more ways for accessing the same set of information. The value of studying a system is not to gain a greater understanding of the system's parts but to learn from the relationships, or interactions, between the parts. It is through the study of relationships that opens ideas up to the various modes of learning. In this way, learning theory and systems theory share important characteristics.

Additional structures found in the Game read like a checklist of education theory stretching back over the last fifty years. Jean Piaget (1896–1980), the father of developmental psychology, had a significant impact on learning theory, specifically with regard to creating learner-centered models. Kenneth Henson, writing in his essay "Foundations for Learner-centered Education: A Knowledge Base," lays out a number of practices based on Piaget's research that include the following:

- Providing experience-based educational opportunities,
- Contemplating the learners' individual qualities and attitudes during curriculum planning,
- Allowing learners' insights to alter the curriculum,
- Nourishing and supporting learners' curiosity, and
- Involving learners' emotions and creating a safe learning environment.

Providing Experience-Based Educational Opportunities: The Game equates *experience* with *discovery* in that players discover, on their own, ways the Game can be changed. In this way, players gain real-life experience of using the world of ideas to effect meaningful change.

Contemplating the Learners' Individual Qualities and Attitudes: The Game is designed to reach a broad spectrum of players, from mainstreamed sixteen-year-olds to undergraduates, law students, and beyond. The design is based on one simple idea per daily Step, each of which is accessible to all. From this simple and accessible point, complexity is added. The energy of the videos is light and fun, and players are left to put as much effort into their daily writing assignments as they choose. I've taught advanced placement students, students recently emigrated from poor countries, Native Americans, and older teens just out of the juvenile justice system. This spectrum of experience has given me the insight to create education models that are broadly accessible.

Allowing Learners' Insights to Alter the Curriculum: The Game's use of Change Orders to facilitate player challenges and the possibility of making changes to the game directly allow players to alter the curriculum in a very real way. Beyond passively allowing learners' insights to alter the curriculum, the Game proactively encourages players to alter the curriculum by awarding a successful Change Order the highest number of points available in the Game.

Nourishing and Supporting Learners' Curiosity: Each daily Game Step includes some current event as a way of demonstrating the Step's lesson. The background of these events is supported by numerous documents and links in the player's My Game Room. If players choose, they can spend considerable time reading the outline, PowerPoint, news links, and PDF articles related to a specific Step. Since each Step has its own web page, players have access to all these supporting documents throughout the Game. In addition, each Step page provides payers with a communal chat wall, where they can discuss related Step issues with other players who are also working on a specific Step—all in the service of curiosity.

Involving Learners' Emotions and Creating a Safe Learning Environment: A very specific effort has been made to make this Game fun. Specifically, the Game seeks to foster a low-stress environment through the self-deprecating character who hosts the daily Step videos. In addition, within this learning model, there is little room for academic or social disappointment. The Game uses a system of work-flow management to prevent the player from building on errors. As long as the player has enthusiasm, everything in the world of letters can be fixed through the editing process. All chat walls are monitored, and there is zero tolerance for unsocial behavior.

Piaget himself said it best when he commented, "Education, for most people, means trying to lead the child to resemble the typical adult of his society… but for me and no one else, education means making creators…You have to make inventors, innovators—not conformists" (Bringuier).

Piaget was also focused on the relationship between learning and morals and believed in two basic principles related to moral education: children develop moral ideas in stages, and children create their own conceptions of the world. Piaget argued that morality is best developed through peer interaction and not through learning from a top-down external authority (Piaget). The Game specifically models this approach to morality through its rules (Codes), which are based on observing the physical world and designed to mitigate the impact of human nature on language. These rules must be justified by the Game itself and are open to player challenge.

Another major player in education theory is B. F. Skinner (1904–1990), who was a Harvard-based psychologist, inventor, and philosopher. Because he believed that human behavior can be affected by small consequences, something as simple as "the opportunity to move forward after completing one stage of an activity" can be an effective reinforcer. Therefore, Skinner was convinced that, to learn, a student must engage in behavior and not just passively receive information.

The underlying structure of the Game specifically addresses Skinner's concerns by allowing players to actively interact with ideas while preventing them from advancing with a faulty product. The Game is comprised of eighty-eight stages, or Steps, where progress from one Step to the next is prevented until the player has submitted an essay to the Gamemaster that satisfies set parameters. Players can go back to completed Steps to reference provided materials and chat discussions but are prevented from advancing out of order.

The Game also mirrors the basic tenets of holistic education:

- Connections
- Flexible pacing
- Transdisciplinary inquiry
- Metalearning
- Community

Connections: The Game is about learning a process for understanding the infinitely complex world of connections. Once two parts of a system connect or interact, a new, third system part, the outcome, is created, in an often-unpredictable process. In this way, systems theory can be described as the study of multiple layers of interconnections that can quickly develop in a nonlinear manner.

Flexible Pacing: The daily video accompanying each Game Step is designed to be created fresh each day so as to capitalize on the "going-on-now" capacity of current events related to energy, war and the environment. Therefore, the best way to play the game is to complete each Step on the day it becomes available. If players fall behind in the Game, they can either stay behind or work their way back to become Step current. The final portfolio project is completed at the player's pace. As such, the Game provides players with flexible pacing.

Transdisciplinary Inquiry: The Game incorporates the numerous disciplines that influence language, including the following:

- Writing
- Linguistics
- Philosophy
- Ecology
- Education
- Physics
- History
- Politics
- Psychology
- Economics

Metalearning: Writing in the *British Journal of Educational Psychology* in 1985, John Biggs defined metalearning as a state of "being aware of and taking control of one's own learning". The Game's use of Change Orders to facilitate player challenges to the game directly satisfies Biggs' call for students to experience academic control. Beyond passively facilitating this metalearning experience, the Game proactively encourages players to effect change by awarding points for their efforts.

Community: A common problem with digital learning is the lack of community created by the separation between students and between class and the teacher. The Game addresses this concern by facilitating community through three different forms of chat walls with various functions situated at different places in the game. There are two general areas where a player goes during play: Player Commons and My Game Room. The latter is oriented toward the individual player, whereas the former is a common space open to all players. The Commons hosts a chat wall where any player at any time can begin or enter a conversation on any topic. My Game Room is fundamentally different, as players can use it to travel through all their completed Steps. Within each

Step, a specific chat wall is internally maintained throughout the Game. Once a player has completed a specific Step, the chat wall for that Step will remain, as will all the other elements of the Step for future reference. A third chat wall exists in a space where players can communicate privately with each other and the Gamemaster. In this way, the Game builds community regardless of where the players are physically located.

The Game and Practice

The Game creates a strict learning environment in the same way that a sports coach creates training exercises within parameters narrower than those found on the playing field. Specifically, the Game requires that all arguments be based on evidence from the physical world derived through the five senses. In this way, the Game forces players to develop specific skill sets. Through the Rules of Discovery (chapter 4), players are introduced to the distinction between the physical world of the five senses and the metaphysical world born of the imagination untethered from the constraints of physical evidence. It is in this context that metaphysics is defined and placed outside of the game without prejudice. Metaphysics isn't "wrong", it just exists outside the parameters of the Game.

Clearly I am not using the term metaphysics in a way that specifically tracks Aristotle's work by the same name. Here, I am using the term in specific juxtaposition with physics so as to create a simplistic distinction between thought based solely on physical evidence, *physics*, as opposed to ideas that begin with physical experience but are otherwise born of the of the imagination, *metaphysics*. Such a distinction is inherently simplistic and artificial, and used for the express purpose of training game players to intellectually perform within a very narrow range of thought.

Think about the football coach who trains players using old rubber tires laid out flat in a pattern. Players are required to run over the tires with knees high and with the balls of their feet hitting the center of each tire as a form of training to improve power, agility and speed. Obviously, there are no tires on the actual field of play. In the same way, Lingua Galaxiae trains players using age appropriate thought structures to promote strength, speed and agility of thought. To use the physics vs. metaphysics duality as an example, there is nothing about the way this game defines metaphysics that prevents a sixteen year old playing the game today from gaining a more nuanced understanding of Aristotelian metaphysics later in college.

Each of the Game's eighty-eight Steps is accompanied by a video generated daily so as to accommodate the use of current events. Each Step requires players to complete an essay of more than twenty-five words but fewer than 651 (the average length of a newspaper op-ed). Before a player can advance to the next Step, the essay from the previous Step must be submitted to the Game-master, who reads each essay and responds with a personalized critique within twenty-four hours of player submission. In this way, the Game turns a major dynamic of digital learning, the capture of education dollars coupled with the elimination of expensive teachers, on its head so that the Game provides each player with daily individualized attention from a trained educator.

On the backside of the Game, the Gamemaster receives each essay and has the ability to make comments back to the player in a distinct field. The Gamemaster can also insert comments directly into the player's text using colored text. All of these comments become a permanent part of the player's database that will be used in composing the final portfolio project. The effective result is that the Game provides each player with a private writing coach.

The Game culminates with a work-product portfolio that becomes the means of assessment. Within a player's personalized work space is a page that holds all player work product next to a web-page builder. The player selects text from his or her Steps and Change Orders and uses them to create a final multimedia portfolio that includes the question "Who am I?" Once completed, the player publishes his or her portfolio, which contains four navigation tabs and a URL that ends with the player's name. This web address can then be used in college applications.

The Game introduces the parts of language in the following order:

The Parts of Language

- Chapter 2:   Change
- Chapter 3:   Self-knowledge
- Chapter 4:   Rules of discovery

- Chapter 5:   Systems theory
- Chapter 6:   Human nature
- Chapter 7:   Rules of language
- Chapter 8:   Language theory
- Chapter 9:   Logic
- Chapter 10: Propaganda

These parts of language are not an attempt to provide a final answer as to what constitutes language, for it is possible that such a question can never be answered—that the answer is itself a process in the context of change, which is further complicated by human nature. My hope is that this effort will motivate others to build competing models. Observe the following and your efforts will be fruitful:

- Thou shalt not discriminate against the inclusion of a system element based on any form of ideology.
- Every act must be in service to the rules and goals of the system.
- Always honor change.

Conclusion

Nothing about the ideas presented here is original. The key point is that teaching sixteen-year-olds about the nature of language and systems theory can be a straight-forward process, no more difficult to teach than general relativity or even Algebra II. Teaching the nature of language only seems difficult because academia has made no effort to make these ideas accessible to the general public.

The cause of academia's negligence, why we do not teach the workings of language, is unclear. One possible explanation is that the increase in overall awareness provided by studying language is inversely connected with the success of advertising and its sister industries of communications and public relations. Entrenched or centralized powers dislike the teaching of systems theory because it exposes who or what they are in the larger context of society and pressures them to decentralize, not for ideological reasons but for the sake of a more successful economy and society.

Chapter Bibliography

Bringuier, J.-C. 1980. *Conversations with Jean Piaget* (B.M. Gulati, Trans.). Chicago: University of Chicago Press. 132

Biggs, John B. 1985. "The Role of Meta-Learning in Study Process." *British Journal of Educational Psychology* 55: 185–212. http://onlinelibrary.wiley.com/doi/10.1111/j.2044-8279.1985.tb02625.x/abstract

Henson, Kenneth. 2003. "Foundations for Learner-Centered Education: A Knowledge Base." *Education* 124 (1): 5–16. http://www.itma.vt.edu/courses/currip/lesson9/Henson2003LearnerCenteredEduc.pdf

Isaacson, Walter. 2015. "How Einstein Discovered General Relativity amid War, Divorce and Rivalry." *Scientific American*. September 2015: 44. http://www.scientificamerican.com/article/how-einstein-discovered-general-relativity-amid-war-divorce-and-rivalry/

O'Leary, Brian. 2012. https://www.youtube.com/watch?v=yO0T05kQkbs&feature=youtu.be

Piaget, Jean. 1932. *The Moral Judgment of the Child*. Glenco, Illinois, The Free Press. 113

Rosenblum, Bruce, and Fred Kuttner. 2011. *Quantum Enigma: Physics Encounters Consciousness*. Oxford: Oxford University Press. 87

Skinner, Burrhus F., and James G. Holland. 1961. *The Analysis of Behavior: A Program for Self-Instruction*. New York: McGraw-Hill. 380

CHAPTER 2
Change is Constant

The only man I know who behaves sensibly is
my tailor; he takes my measurements anew each
time he sees me. The rest go on with their old
measurements and expect me to fit them.
GEORGE BERNARD SHAW, *MAN AND SUPERMAN*

There is only one absolute-sounding statement in the game, Game Code # 1: "The physical world is in a constant state of change." The constant nature of change is the single most important attribute of the physical world, and yet it is the least discussed concept within education. This is understandable given the direct correlation between unchanging truth and power, be it academic or political. Without the notion of an unchanging truth, by what authority does any individual or group claim power? The relationship between change and power is fundamental to understanding language. As will be discussed in chapter 8, "Language Theory," even the act of language is an attempt to capture and then convert change into power.

The unique nature of Code # 1 is itself a lesson. Such a universal statement can only be uttered from the perspective of an omnipotent being that is simultaneously aware of all things at all times. This kind of thinking is outlawed by the Game. The problem with such a position is that as long as we cannot explain gravity and need to use placeholder labels, such as "dark matter," to describe the majority of mass in the universe, we can lay no claim to understanding the nature of existence as a whole. However, when the same idea is rephrased as "Change in the physical world is constant as there are no known examples of stasis," the same idea is communicated but in such a way that it requires continued thought. By contrast, "Change is constant in all things" tends to shut down the thought process. One way to address this conflict in the classroom is to put both statements on the board and have a discussion about how they are different.

The pre-Socratic Greek philosopher Heraclitus (c. 535–475 BCE) was famous for his insistence on ever-present change in the universe. In Plato's Cratylus, Socrates says, "Heraclitus is supposed to say that all things are in motion and nothing at rest; he compares them to the stream of a river, and says that you cannot go into the same water twice." Heraclitus, however, was certainly not the only significant figure to make such an observation. Other such figures and their observations include the following:

- Marcus Aurelius (121–180 CE), Roman emperor from 161 to 180 CE. Aurelius was the last of the Five Good Emperors and was also considered to be one of the most important Stoic philosophers:

  > "Nature which governs the whole will soon
  > change all things which thou seest, and out
  > of their substance will make other things, and
  > again other things from the substance of them,
  > in order that the world maybe ever new."
  > *MEDITATIONS*

- Francis Bacon (1561–1626 CE), English philosopher, statesman, scientist, jurist, and the father of empiricism:

  > "He that will not apply new remedies must expect
  > new evils; for time is the greatest innovator."
  > "OF INNOVATION," *ESSAYS* (1597)

- Edmund Burke (1729–1797 CE), an Irish statesman, author, orator, political theorist, and philosopher:

  > "A state without the means of some change is
  > without the means of its conservation."
  > *REFLECTIONS ON THE REVOLUTION IN FRANCE* (1790)

- William Blake (1757–1827 CE), an English poet, painter, and printmaker:

> "The man who never alters his opinion is like standing water, and breeds reptiles of the mind."
> A MEMORABLE FANCY—THE MARRIAGE OF
> HEAVEN AND HELL (1790–1793)

- Henry Wadsworth Longfellow (1807–1882 CE), an American poet and educator:

> "Turn, turn, my wheel! All things must change
> To something new, to something strange;
> Nothing that is can pause or stay;
> The moon will wax, the moon will wane,
> The mist and cloud will turn to rain,
> The rain to mist and cloud again,
> To-morrow be to-day."
> KÉRAMOS (1878)

- Charles Darwin (1809–1882 CE), an English naturalist and geologist, best known for his contributions to evolutionary theory and authorship of *On the Origin of Species*:

> "We are always slow in admitting any great change of which we do not see the intermediate steps."
> ON THE ORIGIN OF SPECIES BY MEANS OF
> NATURAL SELECTION (1859)

- Shunryu Suzuki (1904–1971 CE), a Zen monk and teacher who helped popularize Zen Buddhism in the United States:

> "Without accepting the fact that everything changes, we cannot find perfect composure. But unfortunately, although it is true, it is difficult for us to accept it. Because we cannot accept the truth of transience, we suffer."
> ZEN MIND, BEGINNER'S MIND (1973)

- Isaac Asimov (1920–1992 CE), an American author and professor of biochemistry at Boston University, best known for his works of science fiction and popular science books:

> "It is change, continuing change, inevitable change, which is the dominant factor in society today. No sensible decision can be made any longer without taking into account not only the world as it is, but the world as it will be...This, in turn, means that our statesmen, our businessmen, our everyman must take on a science fictional way of thinking."
>
> ASIMOV ON SCIENCE FICTION (1981)

Converting the above quotes into individual PowerPoint slides makes for effective class time. Showing how the same idea has traveled throughout time, place, and culture provides that idea with authenticity, which is directly tied to learning.

Rule # 1
The physical world is in a constant state of change.

Championing the ever-present nature of change is a great place for the Game to begin. This is because most students, having grown up in a world dominated by adult power structures that rely on unchanging ideology, will disagree that change is ever present and will look for ways to push back by providing examples of an unchanging world. Therefore, it is important to first talk about the various kinds and degrees of change.

The Game uses a rock to introduce the notion of change. No matter how long you hold one and stare at it, a rock yields no apparent evidence of change. After all, we construct buildings out of stone because we want to create structural permanence. Furthermore, everyone can see that the mountains aren't going anywhere. But, of course, the simple fact is that rocks and their parent mountains are anything but unchanging.

Rocks demonstrate change in numerous ways. A geologist can weave a very long and complex story based on the analysis of a single rock. A granite river rock tells the story of all the processes that went into shaping that rock: the cooling and solidification of liquid magma, the formation of a mountain through the movement of tectonic plates, and the subsequent reshaping of pieces as they are smoothed and rounded while rolling down mountain streams. Eventually these rocks will be worn down to nothing, leaving behind only a trail of sand.

Then, there are the very small, quick changes that happen at the atomic level of the rock. A subatomic physicist can explain how the rock's matter is made up of atoms composed mostly of empty space. Electrons orbit around the nucleus of these atoms and change location at such a speed that we can only determine where the electron has been, not where it is now. The changing nature of a rock may be slow in terms of its formation, but, at the same time, the rock's electrons and related subatomic particles are never at rest. They are constantly moving and constantly changing in a way that is not visible to the naked eye.

Quantum theory adds an additional layer to the story of change. We know from experience and Newtonian physics that large objects in motion, like boulders, will eventually stop moving and come to rest due to the forces of friction and gravity. But Newton's laws only work for large objects. Quantum physics, on the other hand, is able to explain both large and small phenomena. It is at the quantum level that change never stops. This never-ending motion at the quantum level is called "quantum motion" or "quantum noise." In August 2015, scientists at the California Institute of Technology (CIT) announced the development of a way not only to see this motion but to assert control over it.

According to ScienceDaily :

> "In the past couple of years, my group and a couple of other groups around the world have learned how to cool the motion of a small micrometer-scale object to produce this state at the bottom, or the quantum ground state," says Keith Schwab, a Caltech professor of physics and applied physics, who led the study. "But we know that even at the quantum ground state, at zero-temperature, very small amplitude fluctuations—or noise—remain."

According to the laws of classical mechanics, the vibrating structures eventually will come to a complete rest if cooled to the ground state.

But that is not what Schwab and his colleagues observed when they actually cooled the spring to the ground state in their experiments. Instead, the residual energy—quantum noise—remained.

"This energy is part of the quantum description of nature—you just can't get it out," says Schwab. "We all know quantum mechanics explains precisely why electrons behave weirdly. Here, we're applying quantum physics to something that is relatively big, a device that you can see under an optical microscope, and we're seeing the quantum effects in a trillion atoms instead of just one." (California Institute of Technology)

Another example of undeniable change is biological evolution. The only way we can see this change is to study species over time. So, like geology, biology provides a seemingly unending list of changes that continue unabated, just at a slower speed than the movement of a clock's second hand. Then, there is the changing weather... The upshot is that change is a physical constant, even if you can't see that change without the aid of a machine or extended periods of observation.

It is the intent of the game that players will be motivated to prove Rule # 1 incorrect by finding an example of some aspect of the physical world that is unchanging. As much as players try, they will fail in this effort but not after a high-quality learning experience. Harnessing students' desire to challenge academic authority is the basis of an effective learning model. Think for a moment about the difference between students' active efforts to prove the teacher wrong and students' passive intake of content through traditional instruction. The Game encourages players' challenge of authority by combining the natural drive for adolescent autonomy with intellectual investigation. When the game makes bold statements, it does so with the intent that players will be moved to rebel, albeit in the service of academic inquiry. Compare this approach to the standard content-learning model that involves an instructor or book making an affirmative statement and the student memorizing this statement, delivering this statement back on a test, and, finally, forgetting what was "learned."

This chapter represents just one of the eighty-eight Game Steps. From my perspective, this chapter could easily be expanded into a week of class time. In fact, if I were in charge, this Game would be spread out over eight high-school semesters.

Beginning the Game with the notion of change lays the groundwork for the next idea: self-knowledge. Like change, self-knowledge is a constant theme throughout the Game. As the Game progresses, more information relating to human nature is made available, which helps to address the processes of introspection and building a positive internal dialogue.

Chapter Bibliography

Asimov, Isaac. 1981. *Asimov on Science Fiction*. Doubleday. 159

Aurelius, Marcus. *Meditations*. The Internet Classics Archive. Translated by George Long. http://classics.mit.edu/Antoninus/meditations.mb.txt

Bacon, Francis. 1579. *THE ESSAYS OR COUNSELS, CIVIL AND MORAL, Of Innovations*. The Project Gutenberg EBook of Essays. http://www.gutenberg.org/files/575/575-h/575-h.htm

Blake, William. 1906. *The Marriage of Heaven and Hell*. Boston, John W. Luce and Company. The Project Gutenberg EBook, http://www.gutenberg.org/files/45315/45315-h/45315-h.htm

Burke, Edmund. 1790. *Reflections on the Revolution in France*, pamphlet, http://www.constitution.org/eb/rev_fran.htm.

California Institute of Technology. 2015. "Seeing Quantum Motion: Even One Day Ripples in the Fabric of Space-Time?" ScienceDaily, August 28. http://www.sciencedaily.com/releases/2015/08/150828142944.htm

Darwin, Charles. 1860. *On The Origin Of Species By Means Of Natural Selection, Or The Preservation Of Favoured Races In The Struggle For Life*. London: John Murray, Albemarle Street. The Project Gutenberg EBook, http://www.gutenberg.org/files/22764/22764-h/22764-h.htm line-481.

Longfellow, Henry Wadsworth. 1878. *Kéramos And Other Poems*. http://www. hwlongfellow.org/poems_poem.php?pid=307

Plato. *CRATYLUS*, The Project Gutenberg EBook of Cratylus. Translated by Benjamin Jowett. http://www.gutenberg.org/files/1616/1616-h/1616-h.htm#link2H_4_0002 Book 7

Suzuki, Shunryu. 2006. *Zen Mind, Beginner's Mind*. Boulder Colorado, Shambhala, 27

CHAPTER 3
Self-knowledge

> This above all: to thine own self be true,
> And it must follow, as the night the day,
> Thou canst not then be false to any man.
> WILLIAM SHAKESPEARE, *HAMLET*

The most difficult and important question anyone can ever ask is "Who am I?" This primary question of introspection is made complicated by multiple issues. Since, as Locke argued, we are a product of our unique individual experiences, each person is necessarily different from the other. In light of this uniqueness, how do we go about discovering the answer to this question? Furthermore, if change is constant, then individuals must also experience change. This raises the additional question of how anyone can truly know a moving target. Most importantly, what is the best way to teach introspection to sixteen-year-olds?

The question of self-knowledge is the second Step of the Game after change, and, like change, it is a constant theme throughout the Game. As the Game progresses, more information relating to human nature is made available to help in addressing the processes of introspection and building a positive internal dialogue.

As with change, the Game introduces self-knowledge by demonstrating the fundamental nature of this idea throughout human history. Ancient Egyptian pyramid inscriptions dating back to 1550 BCE read in part: "You are one who knows yourself" and "Man, know thyself, and thou shalt know the Gods" (Allen). Other examples include the following:

- Thales of Miletus (c. 624–546 BCE), a pre-Socratic Greek philosopher from Asia Minor and one of the Seven Sages of Greece. He was considered by Aristotle and others to be the first philosopher in the Greek tradition:

> "The most difficult thing in life is to know yourself."
> SOUTHGATE

- Confucius (551–479 BCE), a Chinese thinker and social philosopher:

> "When we see men of a contrary character, we should turn inwards and examine ourselves."
> THE ANALECTS, BOOK FOUR

- The *Upanishads* (seventh to sixth centuries BCE), a collection of texts central to the philosophical concepts of Hinduism:

> "One cannot attain the ever-existent, permanent wealth of Self-Knowledge through and by the use of temporary, illusory objects that you see in the daily life of the materialistic world."
> KATHA UPANISHAD

The above quotes represent four continents and four distinct traditions—all focused on the importance of introspection. The following chronological list of thinkers also reflects a variety of ways to speak about introspection and knowledge of self:

- Plato (424–347 BCE), a classical Greek philosopher, mathematician, student of Socrates, writer of philosophical dialogues, and founder of the Academy in Athens (the first institution of higher learning in the Western world):

> "... in every man there is an eye of the soul which, when by other pursuits lost and dimmed, is by these purified and re-illumined; and is more precious far than ten thousand bodily eyes, for by it alone is truth seen."
> THE REPUBLIC, BOOK VII

- Ibn Arabi (1165–1240 CE), a Berber from North Africa. Arabi was an Islamic mystic, philosopher, poet, sage, and saint, and is considered one of the world's great spiritual teachers:

> "My voyage was only in myself, and only pointed to myself. This is a journey to increase knowledge and open the eye of understanding."
> THE MECCAN ILLUMINATIONS (MORRIS)

- Francesco Petrarca (1304–1374 CE), an Italian scholar and poet, often called the "Father of Humanism":

> "If it is denied to me to search out these hiding places of nature and to know their secrets, I shall be satisfied with knowing myself. It is here that I shall be open-eyed and fix my gaze."
> EPISTOLAE FAMILIARES: LE FAMILIARI (1359)

- Michel de Montaigne (1533–1592 CE), one of the most influential writers of the French Renaissance:

> "No one since has followed the track: 'tis a rugged road, more so than it seems, to follow a pace so rambling and uncertain, as that of the soul; to penetrate the dark profundities of its intricate internal windings; to choose and lay hold of so many little nimble motions; 'tis a new and extraordinary undertaking, and that withdraws us from the common and most recommended employments of the world. 'Tis now many years since that my thoughts have had no other aim and level than myself, and that I have only pried into and studied myself: or, if I study any other thing, 'tis to apply it to or rather in myself… There is no description so difficult, nor doubtless of so great utility, as that of a man's self."
> LES ESSAIS (1580)

- Miguel de Cervantes (c. 1547–1616 CE), a Spanish novelist, poet, playwright, and author of *Don Quixote*, considered the first modern European novel:

> "…thou must keep in view what thou art, striving to know thyself,

the most difficult thing to know that the mind can imagine. If thou knowest thyself, it will follow thou wilt not puff thyself up like the frog that strove to make himself as large as the ox; if thou dost, the recollection of having kept pigs in thine own country will serve as the ugly feet for the wheel of thy folly."
Don Quixote de la Mancha (1605)

- Alexander Pope (1688–1744 CE), an eighteenth-century English poet, best known for his satirical verse and for his translation of Homer:

"Know, then, thyself, presume not God to scan;
The proper study of mankind is man.
Placed on this isthmus of a middle state,
A being darkly wise, and rudely great."
An Essay on Man; Moral Essays and Satires "Epistle II" (1733)

- Ralph Waldo Emerson (1803–1882 CE), an American essayist, lecturer, and poet who led the transcendentalist movement of the mid-nineteenth century:

"Wherever we go, whatever we do, self is
the sole subject we study and learn."
Journals and Miscellaneous Notebooks (1819–1822)

- William James (1842–1910 CE), an American philosopher, psychologist, educator, and trained physician:

"In its widest possible sense, however, a man's Self is the sum total of all that he can call his, not only his body and his psychic powers, but his clothes and his house, his wife and children, his ancestors and friends, his reputation and works, his lands and horses, and yacht and bank-account. All these things give him the same emotions. If they wax and prosper, he feels triumphant; if they dwindle and die away, he feels cast down."
The Principles of Psychology (1890)

- Friedrich Nietzsche (1844–1900 CE), a German philosopher, cultural critic, poet, composer, and Latin and Greek scholar:

> "So we are necessarily strangers to ourselves, we do not comprehend ourselves, we have to misunderstand ourselves, for us the law "Each is furthest from himself" applies to all eternity— we are not "men of knowledge" with respect to ourselves."
> ON THE GENEALOGY OF MORALITY (1887)

- Hermann Hesse (1877–1962 CE), a German-Swiss poet, novelist (*Steppenwolf, Siddhartha*), painter, and winner of the 1946 Nobel Prize in Literature:

> "Because Demian would have demanded more of me than my parents demanded, much more… he would have to make me more self-reliant. Oh, I know it today: nothing in the world is more repugnant to a man [or woman] than following the path that leads to himself! Never the less, about a half-year later, on a walk with my father, I asked him what was to be thought of some people's declaration that Cain was better than Able."
> DEMIAN (1919)

- Aldous Leonard Huxley (1894–1963 CE), an English writer best known for his novels, including *Brave New World*:

> "In its origins [ignorance] is voluntary; for by introspection and by listening to other people's judgements of our character we can all, if we so desire, come to a very shrewd understanding of our flaws and weaknesses and the real, as opposed to the avowed and advertised, motives of our actions. If most of us remain ignorant of ourselves, it is because self-knowledge is painful and we prefer the pleasures of illusion."
> THE PERENNIAL PHILOSOPHY (1945)

In his 1948 book, *Theory of Experimental Inference*, Charles West Churchman discusses the notion that self-discovery is neither linear nor simple. Churchman was an American philosopher and systems scientist known for his pioneering work in operations research, system analysis, and ethics. Church-man describes the process of self-knowledge in this way:

> The individuation process, as the way of development and maturation of the psyche, does not follow a straight line, nor does it always lead on-wards and upwards. The course it follows is rather "stadial," consisting of progress and regress, flux and stagnation in alternating sequence. Only when we glance back over a long stretch of the way can we notice the development. If we wish to mark out the way somehow or other, it can equally well be considered a "spiral," the same problems and motifs occurring again and again on different levels.

Note how Churchman observes that the quest for self-knowledge is not a *thing* to be achieved but a process that never ends. To make matters worse, the struggle for self-knowledge can sometimes be painful. Therefore, it is crucial for students to understand that discovering the self is truly a lifelong process filled with twists and turns.

Besides running through a list of quotes, how do you start teens on the path to self-discovery? Step Two of the Game approaches self-discovery through the question "How do I respond to vulnerability outside of myself?" Is vulnerability in others and nature an *opportunity* to exploit, or is it a *responsibility* to nurture? Teachers can make this an open class discussion by looking at how the notion of vulnerability is addressed in football and warfare, where taking advantage of another's vulnerability is the key to success. How does exploiting vulnerability out on the playing fields and battlefields differ from the best way to organize a society? Can a society that relies on the exploitation of vulnerability from within itself survive in the long term?

Because students are likely to encounter obstacles along the path to self-discovery, it is important to begin on a positive note. One way to sell the idea of self-knowledge is to stress how this knowledge can make decision-making easier. Once the process of introspection is underway and students have a working idea of "Who am I?", the next idea to introduce is the way this awareness can be used as a decision-making filter. In this way, self-knowledge becomes a form of power; instead of looking outside of the self and wondering what other people might think about a decision, the decision-making process becomes an extension of the self wherein the answer is not to wonder but simply to ask.

To motivate students past the obstacles of introspection, ask them if they want to be a passive participant in life, accepting what they are given, or to be an active participant, aware of themselves and their environment? The key message is that awareness equals power, whereas ignorance through passive indifference leaves you exposed to those who seek access to your wallet and your vote.

While some instructors may feel that having classroom discussions about self-knowledge is impractical, the first step is to get the class under control so that such discussions can take place. For me, it once took the whole first semester to get the members of an all-Latino-immigrant ninth-grade class to sit quietly and raise their hands to enter the conversation. Although it took a while, the class eventually reached the point where ideas could be discussed. Then I got smart and began bringing in community grandmothers to sit in the back of the room with the class roster and a cell phone. It usually only took one phone call to a parent at work for the class to become orderly and able to carry on an open discussion that would have made Socrates proud. From my perspective, if students are not engaged in an open discussion for at least some part of the class time, the classroom is not living up to its full potential. The teacher should create a space for this to happen, even in the most difficult situations involving student poverty.

I appreciate the enormous task it is to teach poor kids, especially when you are one of the few teachers in the school who is still trying. When teachers feel that they are single-handedly trying to instill understanding and discipline, it can lead to significant levels of teacher burnout. As a result, the good teachers stay and survive by asserting seniority and only teaching the best kids, while the average teacher succumbs to burnout, which leaves the majority of kids with a revolving door of inexperienced teachers. Certainly, there would be less teacher burnout if class sizes were smaller, which would, in turn, lead to more experienced teachers staying in the profession. Studies on the impact of class size have tended to focus on measuring irrelevant short-term parameters that fail to take in the bigger picture. The fact is that it is expensive to meaningfully address the impacts of poverty.

The present-day science of neurology looks at self-knowledge from a perspective that is fundamentally different from the ideas expressed in the above quotes and from the focus of the Game. Neuroscience studies how we analyze our inner thoughts through *metacognition*, the study of how good we are at judging the veracity of our understandings about the outside world; in retrospect, was our judgment correct or incorrect?

The search for self-discovery, as discussed in the above quotes and in the context of the Game, is fundamentally different from metacognition because self-discovery is a lonely act that is all but indifferent to the outside world. When successful, self-discovery is dominated by the forces of honesty and integrity regarding matters internal to the self. When the above thinkers talk about the struggles for self-knowledge, they are speaking about matters far more sublime than effective tools for climbing the corporate ladder offered by metacognition. Look at how many of the above thinkers speak of the pain associated with self-discovery. Meanwhile, articles in scientific journals discussing metacognition makes no such observation.

The internal struggle for self-discovery is of biblical proportions; this is Saul's trip to Damascus—a struggle so successful that he even got a new name and vocation for his efforts, along with the authority to tell the disciples of Christ (including Christ's brothers) that they never knew Him.

But the pain and suffering associated with self-discovery is not all bad because answering the question of "Who am I?" is the key to language and personal power. Self-exploration is the act of cultivating the inner self, or the soul; it is a form of cleaning house and getting its contents in order. Or, as Buckminster Fuller says, "God to me, it seems, is a verb not a noun, proper or improper; is the articulation not the art."

Rule # 2
The essence of knowledge is self-knowledge (Plato).

While all of the above is interesting, how exactly is a teacher supposed to teach self-knowledge to sixteen-year-old students? To do so, teachers may wish to introduce a list of factors influencing introspection, such as the following:

1. The conscious mind
2. The unconscious mind
3. The role of memory
4. External manipulation

All of these ideas will be discussed in greater detail later in the Game, but for now the point is to introduce these ideas as general themes. Our overall sense of awareness is a system whereby we are conscious of some parts yet unconscious of others. The more honest the process of self-discovery, the more the unconscious self is understood, which leads to greater personal awareness. Some elements in our unconscious may be accessible over time, whereas others may remain inaccessible, regardless of how hard we try to understand their influence.

The notion of the unconscious mind might lead some to ask, are we being driven by invisible forces? Of course we are. But, these forces change, and we change; so the quest to discover the elusive on the way to discovering the self is never ending. Compounding the path to self-knowledge are the ways in which memories are intertwined with both the conscious and unconscious mind. Memories, as will be discussed in chapter 5, and human nature are fickle things that are themselves shaped by unconscious forces. Even when we think we are accounting for all influences, there are still unaccounted forces at play.

Also, it is important to remember that others may attempt to access and manipulate our unconscious through priming and other techniques. Included in this effort to access our subconscious is the desire to influence our overall self-identity. So, the takeaway is get to know more about yourself, including your unconscious, or it will be easier for others to take advantage of you.

We will look more closely at the psychological concept of "priming" later in chapter 10 and will discuss how the industries of advertising, marketing, and public-relations attempt to manipulate our unconscious on behalf of those who pay. This potential to be primed by others who seek to manipulate us is inversely related to self-knowledge because priming is dependent on ignorance.

Remember, the Game is not attempting to provide an academic overview of psychology but an introduction to the very personal process of introspection.

To introduce the notion of the unconscious influence on introspection, all that is needed is the statement:

> There are some aspects of ourselves that we are aware of and other aspects that we are not. Through a healthy interpersonal life, some of the unconscious influences can be moved over to the conscious side of awareness. As such, having respect for the unknown is a valuable interpersonal tool.

Teaching self-discovery defies standard teaching models because it acknowledges that we are all different and that the truth of self is subject to change. As such, teaching self-discovery and meaning is necessarily about sharing tools and techniques rather than about presenting content to be disseminated, consumed, and regurgitated.

When teaching self-discovery, I start with the related topic of love. Teachers can ask students the question "Do you love yourself?" However, make sure, as the teacher, you have already posed the same question to yourself; if students ask, you don't want to appear flat-footed. Follow up with the question "Why?" If you love yourself, then explain. If you don't love yourself, then also explain.

The Game is particularly attuned to the value of self-discovery because of the role played by self-awareness in the function of language.

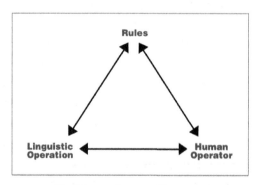

The Primary System of Language

This graphic demonstrates how language functions as collective parts of a system. An essential part of this language system is the Human Operator.

Therefore, who we are directly influences the operation of language. If we are passively unaware of our inner selves, we are the passive operators of language. As such, we become an easy mark for those looking to take our money and vote.

The last part of introducing the concept of self-knowledge is to answer the question "Where do I find meaning?" As with any good education model, it is reasonable to expect that beginning with the question "Who am I?" will prompt students to ask "Why should I care?" Part of that answer is directly tied to the Game's sales pitch, "Play the Game, and you will become more powerful." So, it is important to formally link introspection with personal power. Making this jump from self-knowledge to personal power is bridged by the idea of *meaning*. It is not enough to gain in self-knowledge; this process must be linked to developing a sense of personal meaning. It is through meaning that the individual finds purpose, and it is through purpose that the individual receives guidance and satisfaction.

Rule # 3
The discovery of personal meaning is the foundation of personal power.

These links between self-knowledge, meaning, and power make it possible to see that spirituality comes from the eternal battle for justice, the willingness to stand against those who exploit for their own gain. One of the greatest challenges to self-knowledge is when our ideals are confronted by the temptations of materialism. This is an old story that is captured in the Gospels of Matthew, Mark, and Luke as the temptations of Christ. While fasting for forty days, the Devil takes Christ to a high vantage point and presents everything the world has to offer: wealth, power, and fame. This is a prominent story because it depicts the tension between ideals and desire—a conflict shared by all humanity. As an exercise, teachers can begin by asking students to list their ideals: what is important to them? Then, teachers can ask whether students would be willing to compromise or to sacrifice one or more of their ideals for the sake of wealth, power, or fame.

This exercise can be made even more relevant by posing the following scenario: would you be willing to accept a brokerage account opened in your name that is invested in the defense industry? Your account would pay one million dollars per year. You would never have to work again, but you would also know that your wealth had resulted in large numbers of people being killed for profit. Teachers may need to explain publically traded stock and quarterly dividends.

How about a brokerage account invested in international banks? According to the former head of the UN Office on Drugs and Crime, Antonio Maria Costa, the four pillars of the international banking system are

- Drug-money laundering,
- Sanctions busting,
- Tax evasion, and
- Arms trafficking. (Vulliamy)

Would you be willing to live off of income generated by these activities?

How about an investment portfolio made up of oil and coal companies? Could you live knowing your money came at the expense of killing the earth? Would it change your attitude if you committed to giving 10 percent of your annual pretax income to nonprofit organizations that serve the victims of your industry? Think of all the good you could do each year with 10 percent of one million dollars.

What about if life presented you with a situation where your ideals were pitted against self-preservation, as in the case of your employment? If you were a journalist and the government was looking to justify the invasion of another country, would you support the war for the sake of your career? Dr. Udo Ulfakatte is a former correspondent for the *Frankfurter Allgemeine Zeitung*, one of the largest German newspapers. In his book, Gekaufte Journalisten ("Purchased Journalists"), he describes how American and German journalists are trained at university and then influenced by both private and public forces to spin the news. In a recent interview, Ulfakatte said:

> I've been a journalist for about 25 years, and I was educated to lie, to betray, and not to tell the truth to the public. But seeing right now within the last months how the German and American media tries to

bring war to the people in Europe, to bring war to Russia — this is a point of no return and I'm going to stand up and say it is not right what I have done in the past, to manipulate people, to make propaganda against Russia, and it is not right what my colleagues do and have done in the past because they are bribed to betray the people, not only in Germany, all over Europe. (Walia)

Ulfakatte is not the only example of journalists speaking the truth about their profession. Former CBC News reporter Sharyl Attkisson delivered a hard-hitting TEDx talk showing how phony grassroots movements funded by political, corporate, or other special interests effectively manipulate and distort media messages. Then there is Amber Lyon, a three-time Emmy award winning journalist at CNN, who said in an RT American interview that journalists are routinely paid by the US government and foreign governments to selectively report and even distort information on certain events. Lyon takes the next step and asserts that the government has editorial control over media content (Wahl).

This struggle between integrity and action is precisely the point of Chris Hedges' essay "The Treason of the Intellectuals." In his article, he criticizes journalists' and the intelligentsia's support of the 2003 US invasion of Iraq:

The power elite, especially the liberal elite, has always been willing to sacrifice integrity and truth for power, personal advancement, foundation grants, awards, tenured professorships, columns, book contracts, television appearances, generous lecture fees and social status. They know what they need to say. They know which ideology they have to serve. They know what lies must be told—the biggest being that they take moral stances on issues that aren't safe and anodyne. They have been at this Game a long time. And they will, should their careers require it, happily sell us out again.

For advanced students, consider the George Bernard Shaw play *Major Barbara*, either in written or film form. In the play, Shaw walks his readers through the complex relationship between ideals and money so that, by the play's end, even the most thoughtful are left feeling challenged.

The Game concludes with each player completing an online portfolio. Each portfolio includes four navigation tabs, with the first one being "Who am I?" If teachers are running a parallel model of the Game in the classroom, they should constantly remind students that this question will have to be formally answered by semester's end. It is the teacher's responsibility to continually tie this question into lesson plans throughout the cycle.

When working through these ideas, consider the question: why don't we teach self-discovery in school? The answer is that to teach self-discovery is to teach personal power to students, which undermines the value of advertising and the ability to sell war.

Chapter Bibliography

Allen, Thomas George, ed. 1960. *The Egyptian Book of the Dead: Documents in the Oriental Institute Museum at the University of Chicago.* Chicago: University of Chicago Press. 126

Attkisson, Sharyl. *Astroturf and manipulation of media messages.* February 6, 2015. TEDxUniversityofNevada. https://www.youtube.com/watch?v=-bYAQ-ZZtEU

Cervantes, Miguel de. 1605. *Don Quixote.* Translated by John Ormsby. The Project Gutenberg EBook: http://www.gutenberg.org/cache/epub/996/pg996-images.html

Churchman, C. West. 1948. *Theory of Experimental Inference.* New York: Macmillan Publishers. 174

Confucius. 500 BCE. *The Analects of Confucius. trans. Huang, Chi-chung. Oxford: Oxford University Press. 1997* http://classics.mit.edu/Confucius/analects.mb.txt

Emerson, Ralph Waldo. 1822. *The Journals and Miscellaneous Notebooks.* Ed William H. Gilman, Alfred R. Furguson, Merrell R Davis. Cambridge, Massachusetts: The Belknap Press of Harvard University, 1961. 153

Fuller, R. Buckminster. 1963. *No More Secondhand God and Other Writings.* Carbondale: Southern Illinois University Press. 132

Hedges, Chris. 2015. "The Treason of the Intellectuals." Truthdig, July 7. http://www. truthdig.com/report/item/the_treason_of_the_intellectuals_20130331

Hess, Herman. 1919. *Demian: The Story of Emil Sinclair's Youth.* Floyd, Virginia: Wilder Publications 2015. 132

Huxley, Aldous Leonard. 1945. *The Perennial Philosophy.* London: Chatto & Windus 1947. 185. https://archive.org/details/perennialphilosp035505mbp

James, William. 1890. *The Principles of Psychology.* Vol. 1, Ch 10. Classics in the History of Psychology, developed by Christopher D. Green, York University, Toronto, Ontario: http://psychclassics.yorku.ca/James/Principles/prin10. htm

Kata Upanishad. 500 BCE. http://vedarahasya.net/katha-2.htm. Ch 2

Montaigne, Michel de. 1877. *Essays of Michel De Montaigne.* Translated by Charles Cotton, Edited by William Carew Hazlitt. Project Gutenberg's The Essays of Montaigne. https://www.gutenberg.org/files/3600/3600-h/3600-h. htm

Morris, James. 1988. *Ibn al-Arabi's Spiritual Ascension.* M. Chodkiewicz (ed.), Les illuminations de La Mecque/The Meccan Illuminations. Paris: Sindbad. p.380. http://www.allamaiqbal.com/publications/journals/review/ aproct09/3.htm#_edn23

Nietzsche, Friedrich. 1887. *On the Genealogy of Morals.* Trans Walter Kaufmann. New York, Vintage Press. 1969. 15. http://www.inp.uw.edu.pl/mdsie/Political_Thought/GeneologyofMorals.pdf

Petrarch, Francesco. 1359. *Epistolae familiares: Le familiari.* 3.1, esp. 14-15, ed. Rossi, 1: 109; trans. Bernardo. Italica Press (April 16, 2014) 1: 118-19. http://publishing.cdlib.org/ucpressebooks/view?docId=ft167nb0qn;chunk. id=0;doc.view=print

Plato. 380 BCE. *The Republic*. trans Benjamin Jowett. The Project Gutenberg EBook: http://www.gutenberg.org/cache/epub/150/pg150-images.html. Book 7

Pope, Alexander. 1733. *An Essay on Man: moral essays and satires*. London: Cassell & Company, Limited 1891. The Project Gutenberg: https://www.gutenberg.org/files/2428/2428-h/2428-h.htm

Southgate, Henry. 1923. *Many Thoughts of Many Minds*. London: Griffin, Bohn and Company. 338. https://archive.org/stream/manythoughtsman00unkngoog#page/n8/mode/2up

Vulliamy, Ed. 2012. "Global Banks Are the Financial Services Wing of the Drug Cartels." *The Guardian*, July 21. http://www.theguardian.com/world/2012/jul/21/drug-cartels-banks-hsbc-money-laundering

Wahl, Liz. *Amber Lyon reveals CNN lies and war propaganda*. RT America October 2, 2012. https://www.youtube.com/watch?v=CFDC7zmJgQg

Walia, Arjun. *World Class Journalist Spills The Beans & Admits Mainstream Media Is Completely Fake*. Collective Evolution. December 3, 2015. http://www.collective-evolution.com/2015/12/03/world-class-journlaist-spills-the-beans-admits-mainstream-media-is-completely-fake/

CHAPTER 4
Rules of Discovery

> Smokey, this is not 'Nam
> This is bowling. There are rules.
> *The Big Lebowski*

Exactly how does one go about discovering what is true? The first step is to account for any assumptions that are part of the thought process. We have already identified one assumption: change is constant. The constant nature of change has significant ramifications, namely that change makes it impossible to prove any universal statement. Positing universal truths in the context of change requires us to present evidence from all places and times—a feat that is not possible for us mere mortals with our limited language tools and busy schedules. Therefore, given the constant nature of change, what kind of knowledge is possible?

While universal knowledge is not possible because of change and humanity's general lack of omnipotence, there is nothing stopping us from looking for knowledge in the moment and using that knowledge to predict outcomes in the future. A simple classroom lesson involves nothing more than a pencil. The teacher stands in front of the class, holds the pencil up for everyone to see, and asks, "If I let go of this pencil, will it fall from my fingers to the table top?" Once the pencil is let go, everyone can see the pencil fall and hit the tabletop. The teacher again picks up the pencil, holds it like before, and asks the question, "Do we know the pencil will fall, or are we predicting the pencil will fall based on past experience?" Ask those who claim that they know the pencil will fall, "Have you traveled to the future and witnessed the pencil falling?"

Use the pencil demonstration to start a class discussion on the difference between knowing versus predicting and the requirements for knowing the future. Essentially, students are saying that when a pencil is released, it will fall in all places and at all times. The ensuing classroom discussion can be used to flush out the difference between universal knowledge and the process of predictions based on past experience.

Since the constant nature of change eliminates the ability to capture universal knowledge, we can begin to think instead about truth in the moment. In doing so, truth becomes a never-ending process rather than a thing in itself, or again to summarize Buckminster Fuller's line, "God is a verb not a noun." This begs the questions: exactly what does the process of knowledge look like, and how does it function?

The nature of truth begins with the nature of evidence. It is one thing to introduce students to new ideas like self-discovery and change, and it is another thing to transition into actually using those ideas. One of the cornerstones of education theory is to begin with what the student already knows and to then move incrementally toward the education goal in a way that never makes the students feel untethered from the lesson's launch point. By the time US students hit tenth grade, they have been exposed to the literary terms *plot* and *theme*. The Game uses these known terms while adding a third term, *linguistic tool*.

In order to avoid the pitfalls of confusing elements of process with truth, the Game intentionally refers to the knowledge-building processes as comprised of linguistic tools. As with a hammer, frying pan, or computer, the emphasis is not on the tool itself but on what is created by using the tool. Like most other tools, linguistic tools require skill, maintenance, and, if found obsolete, replacement. In this way, linguistic tools are seen as vehicles for understanding that require constant evaluation of both the tool and operator rather than as elements of truth to be memorized and otherwise left unchallenged.

The first linguistic tool of the game is *duality*. Adults will see this term and react by assuming that the Game is advocating dualism, which is not the case. Rather, the game defines duality as a game tool that studies the *relationship* between two distinct ideas by simultaneously investigating their differences and similarities (i.e., compare and contrast). In this way, duality is not an ideological or universally true concept but a simple tool of learning.

47

The Game uses the duality of plot versus theme as an entry portal to learning. If a class is comprised of immigrant sixteen-year-olds from undeveloped countries, as I experienced in Los Angeles, it may be more effective for teachers to use something simple and non-intimidating, like a single-frame cartoon, to demonstrate the relationship of these two ideas. For just this purpose, I am still waiting for Gary Larson to release his work, *The Far Side* comics. For more advanced students, it is worth using a recognized novel like *Huckleberry Finn* as the demonstration text. Using a T-graph with plot on the left and theme on the right, students can suggest single words to help describe elements of plot and single words to identify the themes of a text.

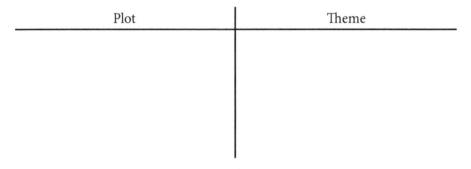

Plot	Theme

The point here is to get students to start using their minds in a specific way to differentiate between two distinct modes of thinking about the same text. Plot describes the questions posed by a journalist: who, what, where, when, and how? This is the realm of the five senses; if it can be detected by touch, hearing, smell, sight, or taste, then it is an element of plot.

Now the classroom shifts to the opposing term, theme, which is fundamentally different from plot. At this point, it is not necessary to say too much about the difference between the two because the process itself will do the heavy lifting. With theme, the single-word terms move away from what can be sensed in the physical world and enter the abstract realm of describing a literary device, reference, or formula to typify or characterize an event or subject. Depending on the level of the class, it will be difficult to think of theme without using ideas best placed under plot. This can be used to the class' advantage, as it provides the opportunity to point out how words suggested for theme really belong under plot. This way, the student still gets his or her suggestion up on the board, while the teacher can use the suggestion to further explain the difference between plot and theme.

Using the story of *Huckleberry Finn*, examples of theme might include racism, morality, and social hypocrisy. Class discussion might cover the difference between the plot's notion of "money" and the theme's notion of "morality." Money is a thing that Huck's drunken father, Pap, demands at the start of the book. Morality, on the other hand, is an idea that typifies or characterizes the relationships between people—an obvious element of the book. In effect, theme contains ideas that cannot be touched or measured with a ruler, scale, or cup; they only exist in the mind.

With the above exercise, the student is learning to think in fundamentally different ways about the same text. Now, the student is ready to move forward and use the tool of duality to investigate the relationships between concrete and abstract and between the sister duality of subjective and objective. At this point, it is important that students not get bogged down by the philosophical minutiae of whether or not there is such a thing as pure objectivity or subjectivity. The point of the lesson is to train the brain to differentiate between modes of thinking.

As with plot versus theme, a T-graph with concrete on the left and abstract on the right can be used to list single-word identifiers wherein concrete represents the physical world and abstract represents the act of creating generalizations from concrete ideas. For example, the characteristics of a soccer ball can be used to build a general set of ideas that apply to all balls, such as roundness, bounciness, and play.

From here, students are ready to look at the duality of finite versus infinite. Again, finite is in the realm of the physical world, whereas infinite defies the limited abilities of language (a matter fully discussed in chapter 8, "Language Theory"). As humans, we can interact with physical objects using our five senses and represent these interactions through language. However, we cannot do the same with notions of the infinite because infinity is a theoretical concept; it is a product of the human imagination that can never be contained by language. Certainly, all kinds of literary efforts have tried to bridge the finite and the infinite, most notably in poetry. But, such efforts can never complete the bridge. In effect, we can experience the infinite, but we are unable to speak of it in any complete sense. Taking the point a step further, language is in fact an obstacle to experiencing infinity. For example, a Buddhist might point out the opposition between language and meditation, where meditation is the act of separating oneself from language-based thought.

Through the above learning process, we are now at our intermediate goal of being ready to discuss the difference between physics and metaphysics and between its related concepts of quantity and quality. These new concepts can be introduced against the backdrop of the previous lessons:

Plot	Theme
Concrete	Abstract
Define	Characterize
Objective	Subjective
Quantity	Quality
Finite	Infinite
Physics	Meyaphysics

The discussion of finite versus infinite is the last stop before arriving at our near-term goal, a discussion of physics versus metaphysics. The relationship between quantity and quality is helpful not only because these terms are likely to be familiar to students, but also because they tie together all of the other previous terms in the above chart. For example, finite terms are ideas based on counting, the act of quantification. On the other side of the scale is quality, which refers to abstract characteristics.

Now we are ready for the final installment: a discussion of physics versus metaphysics. This duality is central to the Game, as it represents a crossroads. The Game is only interested in the relationship between language and the demonstrable physical world; consequently, metaphysics, which relates to the nonphysical world, is placed outside of the Game without prejudice.

As metaphysics is sequestered outside of the Game, the "truth" of physics takes on a huge responsibility. If change is constant, as the Game proposes, then how can physics produce truth? The answer is that physics can only function as a process for demonstrating truth in the moment: Truth + Change = Process.

Look how far the lesson, while incorporating terms students are already familiar with, has progressed in just a few short steps. Truth is a moving target, not because of some metaphysical dream but because truth is understood as a product of the moment in the context of change. This requires no mirrors, faith, or magic: just transparent thinking, which gives everyone equal access to the conversation.

Rule # 4
Truth in the context of change requires a never-ending process.

The process of discovery outlined here draws upon the work of one of the greatest minds of the twentieth century, Karl Popper. In his book, *The Logic of Scientific Discovery*, Popper observes that "whenever we propose a solution to a problem, we ought to try as hard as we can to overthrow our solution, rather than defend it." Popper is a patron saint of the Game because of the ways in which his ideas demonstrate his understanding of human nature as it relates to the processes of science.

Since the inquiry of the Game is solely focused on the relationship between language and the physical world, players need tools with which to test an idea to determine whether it is of the physical or metaphysical world. The Game groups these tools under the banner of "The Rules of Discovery," which includes the **Steps** of Discovery and the **Tests** of Discovery. The Steps help to organize statements, while the Tests ensure the integrity of the evidence.

As with all other aspects of the Game, the process of discovery is understood as a tool represented as a series of Steps. Most will recognize these first four Steps as coming from the study of logic; they are also familiar from the disciplines of science and law. These four Steps of Discovery are as follows:

1. **Construct** an affirmative statement;
2. **Collect** relevant physical evidence;
3. **Analyze** data; and
4. **Adjust** the affirmative statement in Step One to conform to the results of the data analysis in Step Three.

There is nothing fancy about the above process. Notice the looping nature of this model. Exactly when does the process end? When Step Four is reached, it is possible that the set of data in Step Two now includes what had been previously obscured. In addition to new elements in this set, existing elements in the set may have changed over time. As this process illustrates, it may be human to rest on past laurels, but the demands of discovery never rest.

Rule # 5
All statements must follow the four Steps of Discovery: 1) Construct an affirmative statement; 2) Collect relevant physical evidence; 3) Analyze Data; and 4) Adjust the affirmative statement in Step One to conform to the results of the data analysis in Step Three.

In addition to the matters covered in the above four Steps, it is also necessary to define "evidence" and investigate the impact of human nature on the process of discovery. Whenever human nature is present, there is an opportunity for abuse. Whereas Plato asked "Who should rule?" Popper fundamentally changed the question to "How do we arrange our institutions to prevent rulers (whether individuals or majorities) doing too much damage?" Political damage can be defined as manipulating language in service to personal agenda. When that personal agenda is under attack, the natural response of a political hack is to assert the four legs of propaganda: divert, deflect, deceive, and deny. Since physical evidence is the enemy of propaganda, the four legs of propaganda often draw upon metaphysics. Therefore, while the above Steps of Discovery provide a functional platform for inquiry, there still needs to be a filter to ensure Step Two, "Collect relevant physical evidence," is not infected with metaphysical ideas or outright abuse. To accomplish this, physical evidence is defined by the Game as that which can pass the following three Tests of Discovery:

1. Can the evidence be **tested**?
2. Can this test be **replicated** by others?
3. Can the evidence be **negated** by testing?

If an idea is able to pass through this juggernaut of filters, it is deemed by the Game to be "physical evidence that is free of metaphysics and abuse."

For example, can the statement "Zeus is the god of sky and thunder and the ruler of the Olympians" pass the three Tests of Discovery? Since the belief in Zeus is based on faith and not on physical evidence, there is no way to test any assumption about Zeus. Furthermore, without the ability to test for Zeus, there can be no ability to replicate the test. And because the basis for belief in Zeus is faith based rather than evidence based, the believer is not going to be open to the idea that such a belief has the potential of being false.

Moving away from the purely metaphysical, readers may remember the exciting news, in 1989, that two prominent scientists, Martin Fleischmann and Stanley Pons, had achieved a tabletop nuclear reaction at room temperature that produced more energy than it consumed. This was a big deal, as it had the potential to forever change the nature and role of energy in society. Clearly, these scientists satisfied the first Test of Discovery: can the evidence be tested? Fleischmann and Pons' assertions also satisfied the third Test of Discovery: can the evidence be negated by testing? I remember the excitement as the world waited for cold fusion to satisfy the second Test of Discovery: can the test be replicated by others? Many tried, but no one was successful; and the promise of cold fusion became a disappointing relic of 1980s science.

Unfortunately, since no one could replicate Fleischmann and Pons' efforts, their high-profile announcement came to be thought of as embarrassing. But, when the Tests of Discovery are understood, one must acknowledge that the public announcement of an experiment's outcome is just part of the process. Without such an announcement, no one else would be in a position to try to replicate the experiment. This misunderstanding of how knowledge is built persists today, as is indicated by the derision from the anti-science crowd, who point to the large number of scientific-journal reports that cannot be replicated by others.

This is not to say that the world of science is not immune from the shenanigans of human nature. In 2015, *Omni* published a list of "Ten of the Most Deceptive Scientific Frauds." The list is somewhat surprising but informative as to the degree to which human nature can distort science:

10. **Galileo** (1564–1642) is considered to be the founder of the modern scientific method. But he wrote about experiments that were so difficult to reproduce that many doubt he actually conducted them.

9. Compelling evidence indicates that **Johannes Kepler** (1571–1630), the father of modern astronomy, doctored his calculations to bolster his theory that the planets move in elliptical orbits, not in circles, around the sun.

8. **Isaac Newton** (1642–1727) crunched numbers to make the predictive power of his universal gravitational theory carry more weight. Scientists have since noted that he "adjusted" his calculations on the velocity of sound and on the processions of the equinoxes in order to better support his theory.

7. **John Dalton** (1766–1844), the great nineteenth-century chemist, reported numerous findings from experiments conducted in 1804–1805 that no chemist since has been able to reproduce. Scientists now believe he fudged his data.

6. **Gregor Mendel's** (1822–1884) 1865 experimental results, which formed the basis of modern genetics, were so perfect that later researchers were convinced he falsified his data.

5. **Robert A. Millikan** (1868–1953) won the Nobel Prize in 1923 for measuring the electrical charge of an electron. But scientists later discovered that he had failed to report the unfavorable results of related research conducted between 1910 and 1913.

4. The **Piltdown Man** is generally considered to be the greatest scientific hoax of all time. In 1908, part of a skull was unearthed in an English gravel pit on Piltdown Common in Sussex. It was hailed as proof of the missing link between apes and humans. In the 1950s, however, researchers used modern dating techniques to reveal that the skull was

actually an ape jaw with part of a human skull attached, which had been stained to appear old.

3. **Sir Cyril Burt** (1883–1971), a pioneering British psychologist, deliberately made up more than three decades of data from the mid-1940s until 1966 to back up his bogus theory on the relationship between heredity and intelligence. He claimed that human intelligence was 75 percent inherited, thereby reinforcing the British class system.

2. **William Summerlin** (b. 1938), a researcher at the Sloan Kettering Cancer Center, colored white skin grafts black with a felt-tip pen to fake the results of skin-transplant experiments in mice in the mid-1970s. He was trying to prove that human skin, if maintained in an organ culture for several weeks, becomes universally transplantable without risk of rejection.

1. **John Darsee** (b. 1948), a heart researcher at Emory University in Atlanta and at Harvard in the early 1980s, falsified data that formed the basis for about one hundred scientific publications on heart disease. The Darsee case was especially troubling because forty-seven other researchers coauthored his papers and never caught on to the fraud. (Epstein)

The accuracy of published scientific-journal articles is a complicated topic because there are all kinds of secondary issues at play; many of these issues involve human nature. John P. A. Ioannidis is a prominent professor of medicine at several leading universities. Ioannidis published an article in 2005, entitled "Why Most Published Research Findings Are False." In it, he discusses the nature of published research, suggesting that

a research finding is less likely to be true when the studies conducted in a field are smaller; when effect sizes are smaller; when there is a greater number and lesser preselection of tested relationships; where there is greater flexibility in designs, definitions, outcomes, and analytical modes; when there is greater financial and other interest and prejudice; and when more teams are involved in a scientific field in chase of statistical significance. Simulations show that for most study designs and settings, it is more likely for a research claim to be false than true. Moreover, for many current scientific fields, claimed research findings may often be simply accurate measures of the prevailing bias.

Ioannidis, however, is also quick to point out that

We should accept that most research findings will be refuted. Some will be replicated and validated. The replication process is more important than the first discovery...When I read the literature, I'm not reading it to find proof like a textbook. I'm reading to get ideas. So even if something is wrong with the paper, if they have the kernel of a novel idea, that's something to think about.

If the test is successfully replicated by others, there is still one final hurdle for an idea to clear before it can be considered to have passed the Tests of Discovery: is it possible for the idea to be negated through testing?

According to the polling group Gallup (Newport), 46 percent of Americans believe in the creationist view that the God of ancient Rome created humans in their present form within the last ten thousand years. Yet, if you were to ask creationists how their belief might be proved false, the most common response would be a blank stare. This is because negatability, the third Test of Discovery, is not part of any metaphysical belief. In effect, if an idea is thought to be true without any physical evidence, it can never be negated through testing. Therefore, it can never pass the third Test of Discovery and is considered by the Game to be invalid.

Some may find fault with this seemly black and white approach to what is and what is not science. After all, what about all the scientific theories for which there remains little-to-no evidence? Good examples abound. There was the ether of the late nineteenth century. Science had not yet realized that it was possible for light to demonstrate the dual properties of particle and wave. Since we could see the wave properties of water and sound, we assumed that light, too, required a medium for travel. Yet, light could pass through a vacuum, so it was postulated that some kind of ether, or "luminiferous aether," must exist. Without ether, there was no medium through which the light wave could travel and therefore no explanation for the nature of light. In this way, ether became a scientific placeholder until the dual properties of light were discovered. In doing so, science put faith in itself as a process through which future discoveries would either reveal the properties of ether or propose a replacement. In this case, as Albert Einstein describes in his very accessible book, *The Evolution of Physics*, we eventually figured out that light acts both as a particle and a wave.

A similar present-day example is the idea of dark matter. For our current models to work, we need to account for an amount of matter greater than what is currently observable. So, we've given this "missing" matter a name: dark matter. Does dark matter exist? The answer would be "yes," in the sense that it exists in scientific models, but "no" from the perspective of discovery—not yet, anyway. So how can dark matter be considered science? How is the belief in dark matter any different from the belief in Zeus?

The difference between Zeus and dark matter is twofold. First, faith in Zeus is born of sheer imagination. There is no physical evidence justifying the belief in Zeus, as much as the Zeus believers would like nonbelievers to think there is. By contrast, there is a significant body of physical evidence demonstrating that, according to our models, there must be more matter in the universe than we can currently account for. In this context, the idea of dark matter is completely reasonable from a scientific perspective. Placing similar trust in the existence of Zeus, however, is not science. As this contrast implies, we can speak of two different kinds of faith: one born of speculative imagination and the other born of observation, physical evidence, and science. In the latter, faith resides solely in the process.

From the perspective of the Game, there is no such thing as a "scientific fact" because the game considers such use of language to be dishonest. Too often the notion of fact is understood as an unquestionable universal truth. Not only is science unable to assert the universal nature of knowledge, as we will see in chapter 8, the nature of language itself prohibits any claim to universal knowledge. Neither language nor science has the ability to be all knowing because change is constant, the universe is infinite, and our linguistically oriented brain is not.

Rule # 6
All evidence must pass the three Tests of Discovery: 1) Can the evidence be tested? 2) Can this test be replicated by others? and 3) Can the evidence be negated by testing?

I am not averse to metaphysics, nor is the Game. Allowing the mind to wander in wonderment is the foundation of creativity. Beyond creativity, I also like to dream for recreation and otherwise do what Freud observed to be the purpose of our design: to run naked through the fields of imagination. But the Game casts out such processes because they are ripe for abuse. Without anything tethering dreams to the physical world, metaphysics can claim any truth it wants. Moreover, when given the opportunity, unchecked power will always manipulate metaphysics in order to assert and maintain control. This is one reason why our predominantly deist founding fathers of the United States decided not to use the word "God" anywhere in the Constitution and why Article Eleven of the 1796 US Treaty with Tripoli states, "As the government of the United States of America is not in any sense founded on the Christian Religion…that no pretext arising from religious opinions shall ever produce an interruption in the harmony existing between our two countries." As deists, the founding fathers understood that believing in a single creator did not require any authority beyond an individual's ability to observe the physical world and to do otherwise was politically dangerous.

The physicist Albert Einstein, like Spinoza, was a strict determinist who believed that human behavior was completely determined by causal laws. This view relies on the kind of universal knowledge the Game considers metaphysical. Because Einstein believed in a causal universe, he refused to accept the *chance* aspect of quantum theory, that God would randomly play with the universe. In letters sent to physicist Max Born, Einstein revealed his devout belief in causal relationships:

> You believe in a God who plays dice, and I in complete law and order in a world which objectively exists, and which I in a wildly speculative way, am trying to capture. I firmly believe, but I hope that someone will discover a more realistic way, or rather a more tangible basis than

it has been my lot to find. Even the great initial success of the quantum theory does not make me believe in the fundamental dice game, although I am well aware that some of our younger colleagues interpret this as a consequence of senility. (Adams)

Had Einstein been willing to accept the chaotic nature of quantum physics, there is no telling where his brilliance would have taken him and the rest of us; but it was his belief in an omnipotent determined order—a structure that would be true in all places and at all times and that is, therefore, of a metaphysical nature—that prevented him from advancing his knowledge and understanding of the physical world. In other words, Einstein allowed the influence of metaphysics to block his progress.

The only requisite for a metaphysical belief is imagination. The problem is that without tethering ideas in some way to the physical world, there is no way to determine where evidence-based ideas stop and imaginary ideas begin. It is this tethering of language to the physical world that gives every person equal access to the truth. So, if you want to avoid being sidetracked, it is wise to avoid anything metaphysical, as it is all but guaranteed to be a distraction. Metaphysics might *feel* right because it enables us to express our nonlinguistic experiences of the infinite, but that feeling does not mean we are able to capture and control that infinity with language. And how we humans love to control!

Metaphysics is not necessary to practice the Golden Rule, nor is it necessary for running a successful human system. Those looking to metaphysics for solutions are searching for a true ideology when all we need is the process provided by the Golden Rule. Metaphysics is great until someone applies language to voice some universal truth, which is then assumed to apply equally to everyone else. In this way, the individual takes a subjective experience, filters it through language, and then claims to have discovered a universal truth. This is nothing short of linguistic sleight of hand, intellectual alchemy; the same mindset that built the Tower of Babel.

Does science have all the answers? Clearly not, but it is also designed to be free of make-believe ideas. It's OK to dream; just make sure that you don't impose your dream on society at large, unless you have something that is testable.

Rule # 7
Thou shalt not use metaphysically based evidence to support any statement.

Violations of one or more of the Rules of Discovery can be found in almost every example of propaganda. Take, for example, the corporately funded group called the American Legislative Exchange Council (ALEC) and its promotion of neoliberal legislation that opposes unions and environmental regulations. Rather than trying to pass legislation through the US Congress, ALEC provides cash and boilerplate legislative language to like-minded state politicians who, in turn, draft their own legislation at the state level. The result is nearly identical laws being passed by different state legislatures (Graves).

One example of this strategy is ALEC's effort to promote a public-school curriculum that denies the existence of global warming. Titled the Environmental Literacy Improvement Act, this specific piece of proposed legislative language would establish an Environmental Education Council that would approve "acceptable" environmental education materials for the public-school classroom. Such a Council would be charged to "actively seek countervailing scientific and economic views on environmental issues." All of this begs the question of what is meant by "countervailing." Furthermore, the proposed legislation would ban experts in environmental science from participating on the board while mandating that 40 percent of the board be economists. In addition, it states that textbook materials must "not be designed to change student behavior, attitudes, or values," nor "include instruction in political action skills nor encourage political action activities." To date, the Environmental Literacy Improvement Act has been proposed in eleven states and passed in four: Louisiana in 2009, Texas in 2009, South Dakota in 2010, and Tennessee in 2012.

At the core of global warming denial is the manipulation of physical evidence. Efforts like those of ALEC, such as attempting to keep environmental scientists off advisory boards while stacking them with corporate accountants, are attempts to control what is considered evidence. According to the Center for Media and Democracy, "More than 98 percent of ALEC's revenues come from sources other than legislative dues, such as corporations, corporate trade groups, and corporate foundations." So, on the one side, we have an overwhelming agreement among scientists concerning global warming (Cook), and on the other, we have corporations trying to combat the science by manipulating public education or, more specifically, by manipulating language so that statements based on science are placed on par with statements based on a desire for greater corporate profit.

What constitutes evidence lies at the core of power. If the evidence is contrived, if it is derived from ideals rather than evidence, the system functioning under that evidence will falter and eventually fail.

Chapter Bibliography

Adams, John. 1995. *Risk*. London: University College London Press. 127

The Center for Media and Democracy. 2014. "What is ALEC?" ALEC Exposed. http://www.alecexposed.org/wiki/What_is_ALEC%3F

Cook, John. 2013. "The 97 Percent Consensus on Global Warming." Skeptical Science. http://www.skepticalscience.com/global-warming-scientific-consensus.htm

Einstein, Albert. 1938. *The Evolution of Physics*. Cambridge: Cambridge University Press.

Environmental Literacy Improvement Act. 2000. ALEC Exposed. http://www.alecexposed.org/w/images/8/8c/3F1-Environmental_Literacy_Improvement_Act_Exposed.pdf

Epstein, Josh. 2015. "Ten of the Most Deceptive Scientific Frauds." *Omni*, July 8. https://omnireboot.com/2015/10-most-deceptive-scientific-frauds/

Graves, Lisa. 2011. "A CMD Report on ALEC's Funding and Spending." PR Watch, July 13. http://www.prwatch.org/news/2011/07/10887/cmd-special-report-alecs-funding-and-spending

Ioannidis, John P. A. 2005. "Why Most Published Research Findings Are False." *PLoS Medicine* 2 (8): e124. doi: 10.1371/journal.pmed.0020124. http://journals.plos.org/plosmedicine/article?id=10.1371/journal.pmed.0020124

Newport, Frank. 2012. "In US, 46 Percent Hold Creationist View of Human Origins." *Gallup*, June 1. http://www.gallup.com/poll/155003/hold-creationist-view-human-origins.aspx

Popper, Karl. (1934/1959) 2002. *The Logic of Scientific Discovery.* New York: Routledge. xix http://strangebeautiful.com/other-texts/popper-logic-scientific-discovery.pdf

Treaty with Tripoli. 1796. *The Barbary Treaties 1786-1816 Treaty of Peace and Friendship, Signed at Tripoli November 4, 1796.* art. 11. Treaties and Other International Acts of the United States of America. Edited by Hunter Miller. Volume 2, Documents 1-40 : 1776-1818. Washington : Government Printing Office, 1931. http://avalon.law.yale.edu/18th_century/bar1796t.asp

CHAPTER 5

Systems Theory

> If Critical Systems Thinking is to contribute to
> enlightened societal practice, it should be accessible
> not only to well-trained decision makers and
> academics but also to a majority of citizens.
> ROBERT LOUIS FLOOD AND NORMA R. A. ROMM,
> *CRITICAL SYSTEMS THINKING*

What are systems? To understand any system is to account for its parts and then to study the interactions between those parts. Take for instance the human body's system of thermoregulation that manages the body's core temperature. The general parts of this system include temperature receptors throughout the body, the hypothalamus, and the various bodily functions controlled by the hypothalamus. So far, all we have done is create a cursory list of the parts that make up the system of thermoregulation. The next step is to study the interaction between these parts. Temperature receptors send signals indicating body temperature to the hypothalamus. That information is received by the hypothalamus, which in turn processes the information and sends out subsequent signals to initiate various bodily functions that assist the body in either creating or removing heat. Temperature receptors around the body continue to update the hypothalamus with new information, and around and around it goes. Through this process, the body is able to maintain the relatively narrow range in core temperature necessary for sustaining life.

The same process can be used to understand human systems. Take baseball, for instance. Baseball is a sport made up of athletes, fans, uniforms, rules, umpires, coaches, beer, venues, contract negotiations, steroids, and the opening season pitch—to name just a few of its parts. But as every fan of baseball knows, it's not baseball until the players' strike has ended; contracts are signed; athletes don their uniforms; fans are in the stands eating hot dogs; and an umpire is tossing one of the coaches out of the game. Think about baseball and all of its complexities, all of the many interactions between the parts which make up the game, such as statistics and water-cooler bragging rights. How much would you understand about baseball if you only had a list of its parts? Not much. Knowledge of baseball only comes from understanding the collective relationships between the parts as a whole, not from analyzing the parts individually.

Like the system of thermoregulation and baseball, language itself is a system. The Game identifies three primary components of language:

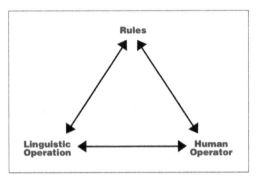

All three elements, rules, operation and operator, are in tension with one another.

Rule # 9
Language is a product of the relationships between the Human Operator, the Linguistic Operation, and the established Rules.

The deficit of understanding that comes from analyzing parts independently from the whole is demonstrated by the Indian parable of the blind men and the elephant. A small group of blind men come upon an elephant, and each touches a unique part of the animal. Subsequently, each man has a different understanding of the elephant based on the part he has touched. One man touches the elephant's leg and pronounces the elephant to be like a pillar or a tree. Another touches the tail, another a tusk, and so on. In the end, none of the blind men understand what he has observed because each individual only interacted with one part of the elephant. To understand an elephant or any other complex system, one must observe the interactions between all its parts.

Richard Levins and Richard Lewontin describe the interaction between parts of a set in the introduction to their 1985 book *The Dialectical Biologist*:

> Parts and wholes evolve in consequence of their relationship, and the relationship itself evolves. These are the properties of things that we call dialectical: that one thing cannot exist without the other, that one acquires its properties from its relation to the other, that the properties of both evolve as a consequence of their interpenetration.

Certainly, none of this is particularly novel. In Book VIII of his book *Metaphysics*, Aristotle observed,

> with respect both to definitions and to numbers, what is the cause of their unity? In the case of all things which have several parts and in which the totality is not, as it were, a mere heap, but the whole is something beside the parts

Along the same vein, Euclid (350 BCE), the Greek father of geometry, stated in his book *Elements* that "the whole is greater than the part."

In fact, this notion of *all the parts* is fundamental to the learning process. One of the classic teaching methodologies for educators is the goal of having students "connect the dots," which is nothing more than creating context—beginning with what the student already knows and then moving incrementally toward the learning objective. Therefore, by looking at the world as a series of interconnecting systems, the practitioner of systems theory creates the ultimate learning context because the process of systems theory begins with collecting all the parts of the system, or all the "dots." In going on to study the interactions between the parts or dots, the systems theory practitioner is connecting the dots and accomplishing the same thing as an educator working through a lesson.

The application of systems theory also substantially increases predictability.

By understanding that knowledge comes from observing the interactions of a system's parts, an anomaly in one part is understood in relation to the impact that anomaly will have on the rest of the system. Well before the anomaly's impact is known system wide, the anomaly alone becomes a warning sign requiring action. For example, while non-system thinkers are waiting for the effects of climate change to parade down Main Street, we system thinkers understand that a 40 percent drop in the worldwide bee population and the dramatic loss of polar ice are significant enough warning signals to warrant action now.

As with all things related to the Game, the point is not to craft a winning philosophical argument but to ask how generally agreed-upon ideas can be brought together and taught to sixteen-year-olds. Since the Game champions the learning of process through practice over memorization of content, the first step in the students understanding of systems theory is to teach them simple procedural steps. The Steps of System Theory are

1. List all the parts of the system;
2. Determine if the system is *open* or *closed*; and
3. Observe the interaction between the system's parts.

Rule # 8
All statements must be built using the three Steps of Systems Theory: 1) List all the parts of the system; 2) Determine if the system is open or closed; and 3) Observe the interaction between the system's parts.

Look how the above incorporates the already discussed role constant change plays in life. Systems theory is not about teaching content; it teaches process by focusing on the relationships between parts. How parts interact today may be different from how they act tomorrow because the context of the interaction may have changed.

The act of listing all the parts of a system is nothing more than set theory and Venn diagrams that are discussed in math class well before our target age of sixteen. Since sixteen-year-olds already know set theory from math class, it can be leveraged and used in the English classroom. Teachers could throw a little history into the mix, give a nod to John Venn, and mention how he was not just a mathematician but a philosopher as well. Teachers could also describe all the disciplines that have adopted his vision of set theory, such as logic, statistics, and computer science.

Furthermore, it is important to discuss how systems theory is effectively a "good-faith" effort. The systems-theory practitioner makes every effort to determine the truth of a set but otherwise accepts that the effort is going to fall short because no observer is omnipotent. The possibility, or likelihood, that an observer will fail to account for *all* the parts of the system is simply too great to ignore. The upshot is that systems theory requires one to have intellectual humility so that there can be an honest understanding of the limitations of systems theory. Given what will be discussed later concerning human nature (chapter 6), intellectual humility is not just a good idea in some ethical or moral sense but is also essential for maximizing the potential of systems theory because of the way humility combats the undesirable elements of human nature.

There is no need to represent unrecognized parts of a set as something negative. Rather, these unknowns can be discussed as something positive and the basis of future discoveries. The entire era of modernism can be described as a process by which individuals identified additional parts of the respective sets that had been left out by earlier thinkers.

Active versus Passive Systems

After outlining the basics of the systems-theory process, the next step is to provide examples of this process that are readily understood by students. First, however, it is necessary to differentiate between active and passive systems. These can be described in simple terms: active systems have set goals and actively work toward achieving those goals, as with thermoregulation; by contrast, passive systems are not capable of setting goals, as a pond is not—an idea discussed later in this chapter. A general line of demarcation between these two systems is whether or not they involve a central nervous system, as in biological systems, or involve the presence of language, as in human systems. Each case represents an active system capable of goal setting.

As with the earlier example of baseball, any sport would equally suffice to describe a human system. Once students have used single-word identifiers to list all the parts of a sport, the teacher can follow with the question "If we were to take all these things and pile them in the middle of the playing field, would we have the game of soccer, basketball, tennis, football, and so on?" From here, examples of sets, or systems, can be expanded to include nonsport-related human systems, such as government, energy, and foreign relations.

Because systems theory comes from observing the physical word, it is easy to keep initial discussions simple. The science of ecology, for example, is largely the product of applying systems theory to the natural world. Much of what systems theory has to teach us can be discovered by packing a lunch, sitting quietly by a pond, and observing how the parts of the pond interact. No special tool is needed, but a magnifying glass and binoculars can augment what can be observed. Returning to the three Steps of Systems Theory, the picnicker's first job is to list the parts of the pond—fish, salamanders, snakes, insects, frogs, birds, water, plants, and so on—and then to observe these parts interacting.

In his 1968 book *General System Theory,* Ludwig von Bertalanffy develops various ways to enhance the observation of interacting parts within dynamic systems like the human body. He argues that there are four important processes within systems thinking:

1. Information and feedback
2. Closed versus open systems
3. Causality and purposeful interaction
4. Life and tension

Information and Feedback: Since systems are about interactions between parts, the primary dynamic of living systems is the flow of information between these parts. In the example of thermoregulation, if the flow of information between temperature receptors and the hypothalamus is in any way altered, if the information is delayed or inaccurate, the hypothalamus cannot do its job. In this way, thermoregulation demonstrates the concept of *feedback*, or information flow, which in this case regulates body temperature. If the flow of accurate and timely information to or from the hypothalamus is altered, causing the information to be separated from its causal link with the physical world, then the process of thermoregulation is broken, the body is unable to regulate its core temperature, and it dies.

Information and feedback are also essential parts of any successful human system. If a board of directors or city council is provided with late or inaccurate information, the decisions of these bodies will be faulty and lead to dysfunction. The constant nature of change compounds the importance of feedback. Without feedback, systems are unable to accommodate change while maintaining their goals, such as balanced sustainability. In the case of human systems, to understand feedback is to understand the nature of language as a system.

I have personally experienced the way the politicization of feedback—when the timeliness and accuracy of information becomes subordinate to a personal agenda—can render an entire bureaucracy impotent. I served the California Legislature in the 1990s as the lead investigator for the committee overseeing the state auditor. My area of expertise was public-school construction. During this time, the Los Angeles school district started building a high school costing $250 million downtown, on top of an otherwise-undeveloped, former wild-cat oil field dating back to the 1800s. The state, not wanting to spend scarce school-construction funds to clean up the environmental hazards left by others, required a Department of Education inspector to visit prospective building sites to confirm that they were hazard-free. In this case, the state inspector was having an affair with the school district official who was overseeing the construction. Although the state relied on the feedback provided by its inspector, the inspector's loyalties were with her lover. Because of the inspector's personal agenda, state funds were released to begin construction in direct violation of state code. By the time I got involved, buildings had already been constructed without any effort to remediate the hazardous gases, such as hydrogen sulfide, that were freely flowing to the surface from an estimated one-hundred-plus improperly capped wildcat oil wells. This failure to respect the role of feedback within a human system ended up costing taxpayers literally tens of millions of dollars up front, in addition to the obscene annual costs needed to maintain the subsequently installed remediation systems. All this happened because the feedback loop had been corrupted by self-interested scofflaws.

Rule # 12
Accurate and timely information flow through feedback loops is essential for system sustainability.

Closed Versus Open Systems: The next step is to ask if a system is open or closed. Using the example of a pond, what feeds the pond with water? Is it fed by a spring or by streams flowing from distant watersheds? Does water simply flow into the pond, or does water also flow out? Does water seep into the ground? Does the evaporation of water from the pond's surface constitute an outflow? Where does the rain come from that feeds the watershed that flows into the pond? Where do the fish eggs come from to give the pond its fish? Questions like these quickly make one realize that the pond does not exist in isolation but is a product of outside forces. As such, this system is *open*.

Similarly, human systems, specifically sports, can be analyzed to see whether or not they are *open* or *closed* systems. What parts of baseball might be understood as representing an open system? Can baseball survive if ticket prices become so high that they are prohibitive for the average fan? Can baseball survive scandals such as game rigging and steroid use?

Causality and Purposeful Interaction: Passive systems have causality where one element interacts with another to generate an outcome. There is causality in a pond when too much nitrogen causes excess plant growth, which sets a chain of events into motion that robs the oxygen in the water and results in the death of other organisms like fish. However, there is nothing purposeful about this chain of events. The pond does not have a central nervous system, nor is it otherwise conscious of itself and the events taking place. Yes, casualty exists in a pond as with any passive system, but there is nothing purposeful about the pond as it transitions into a bog because of too much nitrogen in the water.

Purposefulness requires a central nervous system. Whether the system is conscious or not is an intermediate question. If a central nervous system is in place, then there exists the potential for purposefulness. The hypothalamus is a good example because the system is able to pursue purposefulness without consciousness. Nonetheless, the hypothalamus system is able to pursue a goal of maintaining a narrow range of core body temperature; a pond, in contrast, has no such ability for management.

What sets the human mind apart from the hypothalamus is that the mind is able to consciously choose and manage its goals. Humans are able to collectively design and maintain systems that are wholly purposeful and not the result of default purposefulness, such as that built into the hypothalamus through evolution. While the hypothalamus has no choice, the collective human mind has complete choice as to how it designs and maintains human systems.

It is this capacity of the mind to make choices that makes the understanding of language so important. How language is used in the design and maintenance of human systems determines whether or not the system will work as intended. If language is used in a good-faith way to accurately represent the physical world, then there is a high chance that the system will work as intended; but if language is allowed to be politicized, to become untethered from the physical world and otherwise given over to a personal agenda, then the human system is guaranteed to fail in achieving its goals.

Life and Tension: Tension is the force that answers the questions of how systems create balance and why integrity is so important for achieving balance. The Greek philosopher Diogenes said, "All things come into being by conflict of opposites, and the sum of things flows like a stream." (Laertius).Take life versus death as an example of tension. What would our existence be like without these two forces? Could there be evolution without the cycle of birth and death?

Rule # 10
Tension between parts is necessary for creating balance amid change.

Integrity

Students have already been given enough examples of systems that they are ready to discuss system attributes. Since change has also been introduced, the concept of integrity is a good place to start this discussion. I like starting big, so the first ideas out the gate are the most important: tension, balance, and change.

These three ideas form the foundation of ecology and the basis of Buckminster Fuller's quote "Tension is the great integrity." This is an even-better quote because it comes with pictures:

Montreal Biosphère, designed by Buckminster Fuller, 1967

The structural force at play in Fuller's geodesic-dome design is an extension of the ancient use of a keystone at the center of a stone archway.

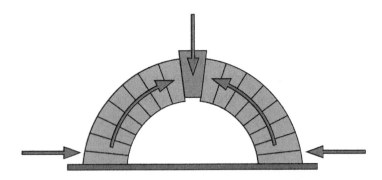

A stone arch is supported by the weight of the arch itself through the redirection of the weight laterally. Fuller's geodesic dome uses the same concept but applies it throughout the whole structure by using the force of triangles. In both cases, the designers are applying the notion of integrity through tension.

Fuller was quick to see the link between the physical integrity of a building versus integrity within human systems and ultimately within the self. Writing in his 1981 book, Critical Path, Fuller states,

> It is the integrity of each individual human that is in final examination. On personal integrity hangs humanity's fate. You can deceive others, you can deceive your brain-self, but you can't deceive your mind-self — for mind deals only in the discovery of truth and the interrelationship of all truths.

By using the example of architecture to describe integrity through tension, students are ready to use the same ideas in abstract applications. Ask students: what is the causal relationship between tension and integrity? How does tension produce integrity? Martin Luther King, Jr., writing in his 1963 Letter from a Birmingham Jail, observed,

> Actually, we who engage in nonviolent direct action are not the creators of tension. We merely bring to the surface the hidden tension that is already alive. We bring it out in the open, where it can be seen and dealt with. Like a boil that can never be cured so long as it is covered up but must be opened with all its ugliness to the natural medicines of air and light, injustice must be exposed, with all the tension its exposure creates, to the light of human conscience and the air of national opinion before it can be cured.

How does King's observation fit into Fuller's broader notion of integrity?

Rule # 13
System success in reaching stated goals requires integrity between rules and action.

From the Game's perspective, integrity is not a moral issue but a necessary component of any system that relies on information loops, or feedback. Be it the human hypothalamus system or a city council, these systems rely on the

73

accurate and timely flow of information. Without such information, no system can adequately respond to change, which is the sole constant of our physical world. And without integrity, it doesn't matter whether a new leader, program or initiative is selected; if system players don't honor the system's mission statement, no amount of policy change will matter. Depending on the level of the class, students could be asked about the impact of failed bureaucratic integrity on the fall of the Roman Empire and the possibility of present-day parallels.

Balance

We have been discussing tension, so it is now time to bring this idea into the context of balance and change. If change is constant in all place and time, what then is balance? This is the point where active systems diverge from passive systems. Yes, there is balance in passive systems. For example, when too-many deer compete for too-little food, the result will be a major decline in the deer population. Nevertheless, nature does not harbor any goals; it just does what it does. To put it plainly, a pond can't plan ahead, is not able to set goals, and otherwise doesn't care if it lives or dies. Nature finds balance without concern for anyone's opinion. Human systems, in this way, are substantively different because we as humans can collectively organize and purposefully set goals based on objectives like sustainability.

Rule # 11
Human systems use tension and balance to create sustainability.

Given our human capacity to set purposeful goals in the context of constant change, what is the role played by tension in human systems? Humans can create and foster tension as a means to manage the inherent imbalance found in human nature. As we explore the following characteristics of systems theory—sustainability, accountability, and transparency—notice how these forces provide much-needed tension and combat imbalance in human systems.

One example of how human systems can be corrupted is the way socio-economic privilege naturally seeks self-preservation to the degree that those with privilege will disrupt the self-correcting functions of a system for the sake of maintaining the *status quo*. Using racial privilege as an example of system imbalance can be a very effective learning tool, particularly in a minority classroom.

Balance: A general quality of systems is that they seek balance as the result of tension. It is important to note that the concept of balance can be romanticized. If a passive ecosystem like a pond experiences an excessive inflow of nitrogen, the pond will seek a new state of balance as it turns into a swamp and then a bog.

Active, and therefore purposeful, human systems are a different story, however, because balance is defined in relation to a mission statement. If it were otherwise, human systems would not achieve balance until there was complete chaos. We only experience social order because we decide to create, support, and maintain order as a social act—sometimes collectively and sometimes through force.

A purposeful human system displays imbalance when elements begin working against the system's goal. When there is social upset, the problem is fixed by locating and addressing the source of the imbalance or by repression through force. The question is whether the identified source of disorder accurately represents the situation or whether the rulers are attempting to create a social scapegoat to deflect and hide their own self-serving acts.

Sustainability: Teachers can start a discussion about sustainability by drawing on the earlier example of the pond. Farmer John grows corn in fields that drain into the watershed feeding the pond. Since Farmer John is in the business of farming to make a profit, he wants to maximize his return on investment by maximizing the number of bushels of corn harvested per acre planted. To maximize his return, he applies herbicides, insecticides, and petroleum-based nitrogen fertilizers to his fields. A portion of these applications migrate away from the farm through leaching into the groundwater or as runoff into the watershed, which eventually is deposited into the pond.

While the pond receives input from Farmer John's fields, the output flow is primarily evaporation. As water evaporates from the surface of the pond, the concentration of herbicides, insecticides, and nitrogen fertilizers in the pond increases. Like the hypoxic dead zone in the Gulf of Mexico that is fed by the agricultural runoff carried by the Mississippi river, Farmer John's pond also becomes a hypoxic dead zone where excess nitrogen creates an imbalance of too much food for waterborne plants. The resulting overpopulation of plants consumes all the oxygen in the water so that no other organisms can survive. In effect, Farmer John's farming practices have resulted in imbalance in the pond; as a result, the pond is not able to *sustain* its former balance and instead becomes a swamp and then a bog. The pond eventually reaches a state of balance, just not the state it enjoyed before all the agricultural runoff.

The above example is helpful because it effectively combines both natural and human systems, thereby offering an instructive segue to discussing human systems. Sustainability is a human construct and does not exist outside the mind. If nature is balanced in the same way for extended periods of time, it is not because of some conscious force. Conversely, sustainability in human systems is achieved through intentional balance brought about by a conscious decision rather than through the default or passive balance provided by nature. In both, imbalance is the enemy of sustainability. Similar to the impact of Farmer John's use of nitrogen fertilizers, a representative government can become imbalanced if money is allowed to trump public will.

Within human systems, sustainability creates positive tension because it is integrated into the human system's goals, policies, and procedures through "purposeful goal seeking." Unlike balance in nature that is attained without conscious input, fostering sustainability in human systems requires conscious intent, goals, and follow-through.

Rule # 19
Successful human systems have purposefully designed goals that foster balanced sustainability.

Accountability: Feedback is the mechanism that ensures accountability. The hypothalamus relies on information flow, but there is no outside force holding the hypothalamus to account. If the hypothalamus fails to deliver, the body dies—end of story. In other words, accountability requires consciousness. In the context of the Game, accountability is a product of the conscious mind and the force that checks the inherent imbalances in human systems that result from human nature (chapter 6).

Examples of accountability in human systems include the broad arena of auditing. We audit our own records, and others do the same. In both cases, the auditor goes back over the records to ensure they are accurate. Accurate records are necessary to ensure that the underlying system is functioning properly and that the system in place to prevent imbalance is functioning as designed. To illustrate this example, teachers could bring in news headlines announcing that an audit has revealed that some person or organization has been functioning with imbalance.

While audits are the initial stage of accountability, enforcement is the next step in holding people and groups accountable. Holding others accountable is the stated responsibility of the press; after all, if the press doesn't expose imbalanced behavior in a human system, who will? Certainly, the individual engaged in the imbalanced behavior won't, neither will that individual's superiors, because the fallout from a scandal has a way of flowing upward. What, then, happens to a human system when the press, the Fourth Estate, is taken over and run by the private interests it formerly investigated? What happens to a human system when accountability is lost? Teachers can ask students what they think about the fact that the US Pentagon has never been audited.

I used to be a very naive person without any notion of accountability. Raised in the country by Christian fundamentalists, I went from the US Marine Corps to Wall Street under the assumption that there was a causal connection between wealth and God's grace. Toward the end of my tenure at the Chicago Mercantile Exchange, I was heavily involved in selling futures to the savings and loan industry to hedge against the double-digit interest rates that were undermining the entire industry. Even though hedges are preventative and not a solution to an existing problem, we were selling these products after the fact, selling junk products to desperate people. We encouraged clients to "trade the hedge," which was nothing but a scam to inflate our brokerage fees. What we did accomplish was to make the S&L red ink look black for a time, but, in turn, we exacerbated and lengthened the overall financial debacle, which resulted in an even-larger tax-funded bailout. After *Barron's* announced that the brokerage industry had captured a third of the S&L bailout funds, I began the process of quitting the industry and was gone two months later. When people know there is no accountability, the worst of human nature takes over.

Rather than improving over the past twenty years, it appears the situation of ethics in banking has continued its downward spiral. Speaking at the Philadelphia Federal Reserve on April 17, 2013, Professor Jeffrey Sachs of Columbia University commented,

> I believe we have a crisis of values that runs extremely deep…I meet a lot of these Wall Street people on a regular basis right now. I'm going to put it very bluntly. I regard the moral environment as pathological. And I'm talking about the human interactions that I have. I've not seen anything like this, not felt it so palpably. These people are out to make billions of dollars and believe nothing should stop them. They have no responsibility to pay taxes. They have no responsibility to their clients. They have no responsibility to people. They are tough, greedy, aggressive, and feel absolutely out of control, you know, in a quite literal sense. (Smith)

Sachs went on to state that today the financial sector is the largest contributor to US politics. For those of us wondering why our socioeconomic systems are broken, Sachs explains that individuals akin to pirates have boarded and captured our economic and political systems. Without accountability, there is no check against this type of predatory thinking and behavior.

Transparency: The relationship between feedback and accountability is a significant issue for anyone relying on human systems. The tool used to investigate this relationship is transparency. As the term implies, if the relationship between feedback and accountability is *transparent*, then that relationship is open for all to see. Transparency is a way of ensuring that those in a position to lie, steal, and cheat the system for personal gain are prevented from doing so. Any time transparency is under attack, it implies that certain entities are attempting to subvert feedback and accountability. As will be discussed later, human nature can be a corrupting force within human systems.

Whistle-blower protections are one example of a system acknowledging the value of transparency. Healthy human systems understand the corrosive force of self-interest and respond by celebrating whistle-blowers as heroes. In this way, accountability uses tension to create balance amid change.

In an article published in April 2015, *The Guardian* newspaper recounts the horrifying sexual abuse of children by French UN peacekeeping troops in the Central African Republic and exposes the suspension of the aid worker who leaked an internal UN report of this abuse to French prosecutors. The leak reportedly took place "because of the UN's failure to take action to stop the abuse" (Laville). When human systems seek to limit transparency, as the UN apparently did in this case, the underlying problems remain unaddressed.

This UN effort to limit transparency is not an isolated situation. Another article in *The Guardian* reports that the Obama administration "has waged a war against whistle-blowers and official leakers. On his watch, there have been eight prosecutions under the 1917 Espionage Act—more than double those under all previous presidents combined" (Ackerman).

Everyone should take note when governments routinely go after whistle-blowers and otherwise limit transparency.

Rule # 14
Human systems must ensure transparency to promote accountability for the purpose of ensuring errors are acknowledged and causes corrected.

Wholeness

The first step of systems theory is to list all the parts of a system. But, how can one have confidence that *all* parts of a system have been accounted for, especially given that the human condition is rife with opportunities to stumble, as will be discussed in chapter 6? Save for the perspective of omnipotence, which lies outside the realm of language, how can anyone be sure all parts of a system are known? The answer lies in the term *wholeness*, which here is not a state of being but the description of a process. Wholeness is nothing but a procedural goal used by the practitioner of systems theory.

The greatest advantage of discussing wholeness is the way it relates to the concepts of context and learning. The more successful one is in accounting for the wholeness of a set, the greater the context and the greater the learning outcome.

Rule # 15
Accounting for all the parts of a system is driven by the tool of wholeness.

Causation versus Correlation

Another tool of systems theory is the differentiation between types of relationships. The third Step of Systems Theory states, "Observe the interactions of the system's parts." Observing such interactions becomes tricky, however, when one fails to account for the difference between causation and correlation. Was the outcome of an interaction *caused* by two known parts interacting, or was the outcome simply a *correlation* of time and/or place between the two parts?

Rule # 16
All statements must distinguish between causation and correlation.

The question of causation versus correlation is an easy matter to explain to teens because it is a right of adolescent passage to be falsely accused by adults of causing some undesirable outcome. For a teacher, false accusation is the unintended result of having a room full of kids in which a single adult is attempting to create and maintain order. As such, any good teacher is well versed in the skills necessary to apologize to a student who has been falsely accused. Yes, little Johnny who has behavioral issues was standing next to the glass flower vase when it was knocked over when the teacher's back was turned, but that doesn't mean Johnny was responsible. In fact, Johnny's only role in the vase being knocked over was his proximity to the event. In short, Johnny had a corollary relationship to the broken vase by his proximity to the event, but he did not cause the vase to break.

The argument against the existence of global warming is partly based on exploiting confusion over the difference between causation and correlation. As will be discussed in chapter 10, propaganda is the intentional exploitation of language. Global-warming skeptics proactively use propaganda to exploit the confusion over causation versus correlation by arguing that "Since humans did not *cause* global warming, there is no reason to stop exploiting the earth's ecosystem," or so say the spokespeople for those busy exploiting the earth's ecosystem.

The danger of not differentiating between causation and correlation in the context of metaphysics is demonstrated by the practice of annually throwing a virgin female sacrifice into the island volcano so as to appease the volcano god and prevent it from spewing lava and wiping out the village. Is there a relationship between sacrificing virgins and a year without volcanic eruption? Yes. Did the sacrifice *cause* the volcano to remain dormant? No. But without the ability to differentiate between causation and correlation, the decision as to whether or not to continue the practice of human sacrifice becomes untethered from the physical world. This is why the Game sets metaphysics outside the Game: metaphysics untethers language from the physical world and can quickly lead to beliefs and actions that are based on nothing more than unsubstantiated imagination.

Assumptions

Another tool of systems theory is assumption. Purely the creation of the human mind, assumptions are a necessary function of the brain in creating an "ordered" reality. We humans need to be able to make assumptions in order to seamlessly function in a world dominated by change. However, assumptions become problematic when they cease to be useful tools and become truths that are allowed to exist unquestioned. Once the transition from tool to truth occurs, we stop accounting for change. Whether we judge such sloppy thinking to be the result of laziness or a lack of understanding (or both), thinking uncritically by way of assumptions is a great way to arrive at a result that conflicts with the system's purposeful goals and planned outcomes.

Rule # 17
Thou shalt not assume. All assumptions must be analyzed anew to ensure they are in keeping with change.

Ideology is a form of intellectual assumption and one of the building blocks of propaganda to be discussed in chapter 10. Ideological ideas are inherently metaphysical from the perspective of the Game because they exist independent of change. Once the mind has accepted an ideological truth, the natural inclination is to continue to believe in that truth without subsequent reanalysis. After all, what's the point of thinking more about an idea that is true in all places and at all times? This is why Test Three of Discovery is so important: can the evidence be negated by testing? Ideological truths are structurally not open to the possibility of being proved wrong because an ideological idea is simply assumed to be true.

Exploitation

Imbalance in human systems can be caused by many forces, but none is more destructive and capable of causing imbalance than exploitation. The concept of exploitation is a tool of systems theory because it identifies a primary force of imbalance driven by the fallibilities of human nature. Exploitation is the use of a resource without thought of how this use impacts the larger system and is directly antagonistic to tension, balance, and sustainability. To exploit is to disrupt positive tensions and results in imbalance and unsustainable actions. In other words, exploitation is a force that is anathema to balanced sustainability. Society tends to look askance at exploitation from a moral perspective, but morality is not needed to call out and identify exploitation as a destructive force.

Rule # 18
Thou shalt not exploit anything except the sun, wind, gravity, and ocean tides.

Teenagers will be familiar with various forms of exploitation. Since systems theory is another way of talking about context, we can again use the example of Farmer John and the watershed where his farm is located. Does Farmer John's farm exist in isolation, or is it connected with the surrounding land, air, and water? When Farmer John uses chemicals on his field, does he do so in isolation, or do his actions have repercussions beyond his farm? If the larger context is understood, then should the actions of Farmer John be considered exploitive? One way to answer this question is to ask whether Farmer John is using resources he is not factoring into his farm's balance sheet. The answer would be "yes," since he is not factoring the destruction of the greater watershed, including our pond, into his profit calculations. In effect, Farmer John is exploiting the ecological balance of the area surrounding his farm in order to increase his profit. In the end, our pond loses, while Farmer John's bank-account wins—at least in the short term.

The same point can be made by looking at the practice of slavery, past and present. Slavery is the act of exploiting labor for the purpose of increasing profit. Historically, labor has always been the greatest cost of doing business. Therefore, it is only natural to devise ways to minimize this "drain" on profit. Given human nature and the inherent drive for wealth possessed by some, there is a danger in every human system of crossing the line between the reasonable concern for the level of profitability every business must obey and the outright exploitation of labor for profit. If a business, and the society in which the business operates, desires balanced sustainability, it must always be vigilant against the exploitation of people and the environment.

Adaptation

Systems theory is all about change, which is why it is a practice and not an assumed ideology. Since change is the sole constant of the physical world, it is necessary for human systems driven to accommodate change through adaptation. Of course, denial of change is a very popular strategy among humans. It can work well for the powerful, as long as the human parts of the system don't mind that they are being exploited and as long as nonhuman resources, like clean air and water, don't run out. But, if the collective goal of society is to create and maintain a system that serves balanced sustainability, then denial is the enemy. Adaptation is the solution to change.

Teachers can introduce the concept of adaptation to a class by presenting it as the antidote to change. Students can be asked for examples of change being denied. Has the denial of change ever been successful? What are some of the results of denying change?

Rule # 20
Open systems maintain balanced sustainability by adapting to environmental change.

Internal Versus External Cost

A balance sheet is the main vehicle for managing any financial endeavor. The balance sheet is considered the unadulterated truth of a business' finances. But, of course, there are always ways to "cook the books." One way that is often legal is to simply leave off debit items that drain from the asset side of the ledger, like Farmer John left off the destruction of the pond from his profit calculations. When done legally, these unreported debit items are considered "external" to the balance sheet. For some businesses, keeping certain costs off the balance sheet is so essential to profitability that to include them would result in bankruptcy. As such, externalizing these costs for some industries is essential—not just to profitability but to the very viability of the business model. Unfortunately, too many of our business schools proactively teach students how to simultaneously internalize profit while externalizing cost as the standard model for conducting business.

Take for instance the oil industry. A good class project is to investigate those costs externalized by the oil industry including extraction, transportation, refinement, and end consumption. What are the costs associated with extraction not listed on the balance sheets of the oil industry such as the environmental costs of oil spills both on land and at sea and the air pollution caused by the exhaust of extraction equipment and the escape of greenhouse gases such as methane? How much of our trillions of dollars in military expenditures goes to fighting in the Middle East, an ongoing military fixation that only began after the discovery of oil? How much oil is spilt and leaked during transportation from the point of extraction to refinement? How much pollution is created during transportation from rail, trucks, ships and pipelines? How much of our military budget is spent protecting oil transportation routes? What is the environmental impact of this military involvement, inasmuch as the Pentagon is the largest purchaser of oil products in the US economy? How much air pollution is created by the refinement of oil? Finally, how much pollution is created by the transportation and end use of oil?

Notice nothing has been said about the significant subsidies enjoyed by the oil industry that come in the form of tax breaks and direct cash payments. For an International Monetary Fund working paper on this topic, see David Coady's "How Large Are Global Energy Subsidies?"

Then, repeat the same process but instead of analyzing the oil industry, look instead at the solar photovoltaic industry (solar panels). As this process unfolds, one of the first things to be noticed is that for solar, there is no extraction, transportation of raw material and no refinement. As a guide, you may wish to use the 2014 report by Lazard, one of the most respected investment houses in the world, which concludes that renewable energy is now cost competitive with carbon and nuclear energy (Crooks).

Rule # 21
Balanced and sustainable systems account for both internal and external costs.

Centralization versus Decentralization

The terms *centralization* and *decentralization* are instructive because they apply just as easily when discussing natural systems as when discussing human systems. Our pond is destroyed when too much nitrogen is introduced, as the oxygen-demanding plants consume all the waterborne oxygen and make it impossible for other species like fish to survive. This is not to say that nitrogen itself is evil and the cause of the pond's demise. The fact is that nitrogen is an essential element for much of life. The problem is not in the presence of nitrogen but in its concentration. It is the overabundance of nitrogen that causes the pond to collapse.

The same can be observed when forces in human systems become so dominant that the system collapses. Centralization in human systems comes in the form of power. Lord Acton (1834–1902) was an English Catholic historian, politician, and prolific writer, known for having an exhaustive library and being one of the most learned men of his time. In a letter to Bishop Mandell Creighton on April 5, 1887, Acton wrote

> I cannot accept your canon that we are to judge Pope and King unlike other men, with a favorable presumption that they did no wrong. If there is any presumption it is the other way, against the holders of

power, increasing as the power increases. Historic responsibility has to make up for the want of legal responsibility. Power tends to corrupt, and absolute power corrupts absolutely. Great men are almost always bad men, even when they exercise influence and not authority, still more when you superadd the tendency or the certainty of corruption by authority. There is no worse heresy than that the office sanctifies the holder of it. That is the point at which the negation of Catholicism and the negation of Liberalism meet and keep high festival, and the end learns to justify the means. You would hang a man of no position like Ravaillac; but if what one hears is true, then Elizabeth asked the jailer to murder Mary, and William III; ordered his Scots minister to extirpate a clan. Here are the greatest names coupled with the greatest crimes; you would spare those criminals, for some mysterious reason. I would hang them higher than Haman, for reasons of quite obvious justice, still more, still higher for the sake of historical science.

Acton is observing the relationship between human nature and power through the actions of some of the most powerful people of his time, in addition to the way society responds to those actions. When the powerful are caught acting badly, society gives them a pass. President Obama gave President Bush a pass for probable war crimes, including the illegal invasion of Iraq. President Obama not only gave Wall Street a pass for criminal fraud but then gave it billions of dollars in bailouts so that the banks today are even more concentrated than before the crisis of 2008. It is as if President Obama never heard of Lord Acton or otherwise studied human nature.

This notion of society giving the powerful a pass for bad behavior is reminiscent of our cultural willingness to sit on Sunday mornings, listen to sermons that warn us about the evils of the seven deadly sins, and then walk out of the church and leave behind everything we just heard. We act as if ideas of morality don't really apply to the real world despite the fact that the bad acts of those in power read like the greatest hits of the seven deadly sins. Even though power corrupts, we as a culture are so quick to believe those in power who say they need more power with less transparency. This is why transparency is so important: because it speaks directly to how power is kept in check.

Consider the game Monopoly and its relationship with centralization. There is only one outcome to the game: one player owning it all. Given human nature, centralization is the end result of power, and it will destroy any human system that allows power to grow unchecked.

The notion that centralization is antithetical to successful human systems is captured by the life work of Louis Brandeis, who served on the Supreme Court from 1916-1939. Raymond Lonergan, writing at the time of Brandeis' death in 1941, characterized his life's work with the following,

> Neither coercion nor flattery could induce him to deviate from the course charted by his mind and heart.
>
> > "We must make our choice," he once said to a younger friend, who appreciated the opportunity to sit at the feet of this modern Gamaliel. "We may have democracy, or we may have wealth concentrated in the hands of the few, but we can't have both."
>
> He was not satisfied with the kind of democracy which gives men political and religious freedom. He demanded economic freedom, too. (Dillard)

Brandeis was a man who understood society as a larger system of interdependent parts and how imbalance due to concentration would lead to the breakdown of democracy.

Given Acton's conclusion that "Power tends to corrupt, and absolute power corrupts absolutely. Great men are almost always bad men," it is relatively easy to draw students into a discussion. Since Acton is making an absolute statement, students can attempt to refute it by example. Students can be asked to provide examples of unchecked human power that did not result in corruption. If students have been fed a sanitized version of US history, they will probably cite examples of great leaders of American government and business who have been turned into selfless heroes by movies and high-school history textbooks. Taking one example of a great "selfless" hero, the teacher can walk the class through examples of how this person succumbed to power. Students can be assigned homework where they choose one individual and dig beyond the popular myth to demonstrate how power corrupts. All this can be made easy by using Howard Zinn's text *A People's History of the United States*.

I used to sell midsized commercial solar systems. During those years I became very active in the politics of energy. From a dollar-invested perspective, carbon and nuclear energy dominate the US market and politics. In addition to having the financial resources to buy the US Congress, the carbon and nuclear industries have systematically engaged in the "agency capture" of all US state-public-utility commissions, despite the fact that these commissions were created to give power to the consumer in the face of government-sanctioned monopolies.

These monopolies began with independent-energy providers doing what most businesses do if they are able: buy up the competition. By the time the government stepped in to regulate, large parts of the nation were serviced by single companies. Instead of breaking up these monopolies and diffusing the political power through smaller competing entities, state governments agreed to allow these monopolies to continue without competition. Understanding the role of competition in maintaining a healthy marketplace, states established public-utility commissions to provide checks on the otherwise-unchecked concentration of political power wielded by a single energy supplier. Over time, private energy companies systematically took over, that is, captured, the commissions so that, today, they are controlled by the very businesses they were designed to regulate. All of this is a lesson about human nature: it is not enough to establish a government check on private power; such institutions must be forever on guard against being co-opted by the very forces they were designed to regulate.

Rule # 22
Centralization that creates imbalance in a system is prohibited.

Unintended Consequences

Systems can be very complicated, especially human systems. Given that humans are not omnipotent, it is likely that any attempt to analyze a system will in some way fall short. Unfortunately, we humans too often believe ourselves to the point where we believe in the truth of our analysis. We believe our analysis is complete both in its listing of parts and in its understanding of how those parts interact. Equipped with such a "complete and exhaustive understanding" of the situation, we subsequently believe we can successfully control outcomes by making selective changes to the system. In doing so, our unquestioning belief makes us blind to unintended consequences.

One classic example of unintended consequences is the story of Australia and the introduction of rabbits. Introduced in 1788, rabbits were brought to the island as a form of domesticated food. But in 1859, a British colonist by the name of Thomas Austin released twenty-four wild rabbits from back home in England into the wilds of Australia for hunting purposes. Within ten years, rabbits became so prevalent that two million could be shot or trapped annually without having any noticeable effect on the population. The unintended consequence of rabbits being introduced into an ecosystem where there were no predators to keep the population in check resulted in widespread species loss and the annual loss of millions of dollars in crops.

Systems theory is nothing more than an incomplete blueprint of how the elements of nature interact. When humans attempt to impose their will on nature, the outcome can be unpredictable. Nature just does what it does without concern for human opinion; nature is change in action.

Rule # 24
Altering one part of a system can result in unintended outcomes throughout the whole system.

Chapter Bibliography

Acton, Sir John Dalberg. *Letter to Bishop Mandell Creighton*, April 5, 1887 published in Historical Essays and Studies, edited by J. N. Figgis and R. V. Laurence (London: Macmillan, 1907)

Ackerman, Spencer, and Ed Pilkington. 2015. "Obama's War on Whistleblowers Leaves Administration Insiders Unscathed." *The Guardian*, March 16. http://www.theguardian.com/us-news/2015/mar/16/whistleblowers-double-standard-obama-david-petraeus-chelsea-manning

Aristotle 350 B.C.E *Metaphysics*. The Internet Classics Archive. Translated by W. D. Ross. Book VII, Part 8. http://classics.mit.edu/Aristotle/metaphysics.mb.txt

Coady, David, Ian Parry, Louis Sears, and Baoping Shang. 2015. "How Large Are Global Energy Subsidies?" International Monetary Fund Working Paper 15/105. Fiscal Affairs Department. https://www.imf.org/external/pubs/ft/wp/2015/wp15105.pdf

Crooks, Ed. 2014. "US Solar and Wind Start to Outshine Gas." *The Financial Times*, September 18. http://www.ft.com/intl/cms/s/0/e8627a7a-3e82-11e4-adef-00144feabdc0.html#axzz3tB3gUU00

Dillard, Irving. ed. *Mr. Justice Brandeis, Great American*. The Modern View Press, St Louis. 1941 Lonergan, Raymond, *A Steadfast Friend of Labor*. Pg 42 http://babel.hathitrust.org/cgi/pt?id=mdp.39015009170443;view=1up;seq=56

Euclid. *Euclid's Elements*. Ed, Sir Thomas Little Heath. New York. Dover. 1956. Book 1, CN 5. Perseua Digital Library, Tufts University: http://www.perseus.tufts.edu/hopper/text?doc=Perseus:text:1999.01.0086:book=1:-type=CN:number=5&highlight=whole

Fuller, Buckminster. 1981. *Critical Path*. St. Martin's Griffin. 92

King, Martin Luther (Jr.) 2000. *Why We Can't Wait*. Signet Classics. 165

Laertius, Diogenes. *Lives of the Eminent Philosophers*. Loeb Classical Library edition; translated by Robert Drew Hicks. Book 9: 8. Harvard University Press (1925) https://en.wikisource.org/wiki/Lives_of_the_Eminent_Philosophers/Book_IX#cite_ref-16

Laville, Sandra. 2015. "UN Aid Worker Suspended for Leaking Report on Child Abuse by French Troops." *The Guardian*, April 29. http://www.theguardian. com/world/2015/apr/29/un-aid-worker-suspended-leaking-report-child-abuse-french-troops-car

Levins, Richard, and Richard Lewontin. 1985. *The Dialectical Biologist*. Cambridge, MA: Harvard University Press. 122

Smith, Yves. 2013. "Jeffrey Sachs Calls Out Wall Street Criminality and Pathological Greed." Naked Capitalism, April 19. http://www.nakedcapitalism. com/2013/04/jeffrey-sachs-calls-out-wall-street-criminality-and-pathological-greed.html

von Bertalanffy, Ludwig. (1968) 1976. *General System Theory: Foundations, Development, Applications*. New York: George Braziller.

Zinn, Howard. (1980) 2005. *A People's History of the United States*. New York: Harper Perennial.

CHAPTER 6
Human Nature

> It is human nature to think wisely and
> to act in an absurd fashion.
> ANATOLE FRANCE,
> *LE LIVRE DE MON AMI*

Lingua Galaxiae considers human nature to be central to language because language does not exist in the absence of the human mind. Specifically, this chapter looks at human nature in order to better understand the way the human *operator* of language interacts with the *operation* of language. Special attention is given to the way human nature can disrupt the accurate and timely flow of information and otherwise open language to abuse.

The Game starts with the question of the unconscious mind before moving on to the more tangible characteristics of human nature. The idea is that through a more complex understanding of the two primary factors influencing the human psyche, conscious vs. unconscious, players will have a far richer context through which to study human nature.

Discussing the unconscious can be a bit tricky because of our confused relationship with Freud. Although Freud did not originate the idea of the unconscious, he certainly popularized the idea. As such, even to mention the unconscious is to align oneself with Freud. Unfortunately, there is a particularly robust aversion to anything Freud within academia where "advanced thinking" is a function of how distant one's ideas are from Freud's. The end result is that advancements in understanding the unconscious have been hampered. In his

1992 essay, "The Psychological Unconscious," research professor John F. Kihlstrom discusses this academic aversion to anything related to Freud:

> One response to this state of affairs is to argue that psychoanalytic the-
> ory itself has evolved since Freud, and that it is therefore unfair to bind
> psychoanalysis so tightly to the Freudian vision of repressed infan-
> tile sexual and aggressive urges, symbolically represented in dreams,
> errors, and symptoms, and revealed on the couch through free associ-
> ation. Drew Westen himself attempted this gambit, arguing that critics
> of psychoanalysis attack an archaic, obsolete version of psychodynamic
> theory, and ignore more recent developments such as ego psychology
> and object relations theory. But, to borrow the language of the Viet-
> nam War, this destroys the village in order to save it. Culturally, the
> twentieth century was the century of Sigmund Freud, not the century
> of Heinz Kohut or Melanie Klein. Freud's legacy is not to be assessed
> in terms of ideas which emerged since Freud died, but rather in terms
> of the ideas propounded by Freud himself through the twenty-four
> volumes of his collected works. Chief among these is a particular view
> of unconscious mental life—a view which, to date, has found little or
> no support in empirical science. And, it must be said, the modern psy-
> chological laboratory offers little or nothing to support the theories of
> Kohut or Klein, either.

Kihlstrom's point is that when we speak of the human unconscious today, we
are not talking about Freud but about all the work that has been done since
Freud. Kihlstrom then goes on to say, "The rediscovery of the unconscious by
modern scientific psychology began with comparisons between automatic and
effortful mental processes and between explicit and implicit memory. Since
then, it has continued with the extension of the explicit-implicit distinction
into the domains of perception, learning, and thought. Taken together, this
literature describes the *cognitive unconscious*."

Kihlstrom then offers the following list of processes that make up the cognitive unconscious:

- Automaticity and unconscious processing
- Implicit memory
- Implicit learning
- Implicit perception
- Implicit thought

To cognition Kihlstrom adds the areas of emotion and motivation to make up the "trilogy of the mind." I would never ask 10th graders to memorize these lists or even show them in class. The point is for educators to feel comfortable using the word unconscious, not as a thing but as a set of interacting parts. The education goal is to introduce students to the general concept that perception of the self and the external world is influenced by many factors. We are aware of some of these influences, but unaware of others. Some influences will never be accessible to our conscious mind, while other influences can be shifted from the unconscious to the conscious.

Rule # 25
Human consciousness is a complex system including both conscious and unconscious influences.

The Game treats the conscious-versus-unconscious discussion as a backdrop to discussing the following five categories of human nature:

1. Fallibilities
2. Needs
3. Emotions
4. Wounds
5. Weaknesses

While attempting to quantify human nature may seem arrogant, remember that the Game encourages players to initiate changes. If a player can adequately argue that a category should be dropped, added, merged with another, or otherwise changed, then the Game is changed. A record of precedent is made, and the player is awarded points.

Human Fallibilities

This group of characteristics investigates the relationships among the following five fallible aspects of the human condition and their influence on the timely flow of accurate information:

- Sensory
- Cognitive
- Emotional
- Social
- Mnemonic

Sensory Fallibility: Christopher Chabris and Daniel Simons are researchers and authors of *The Invisible Gorilla and Other Ways Our Intuitions Deceive Us*. (The quickest way to get a sense of this book is to watch one or more of the videos at http://www.theinvisiblegorilla.com/videos.html)

According to the book's authors,

> Reading our book will make you *less* sure of yourself—and that's a good thing. In *The Invisible Gorilla*, we use a wide assortment of stories and counterintuitive scientific findings to reveal an important truth: Our minds don't work the way we think they do. We think we see ourselves and the world as they really are, but we're actually missing a whole lot.
>
> We combine the work of other researchers with our own findings on attention, perception, memory, and reasoning to reveal how faulty intuitions often get us into trouble. In the process, we explain the following:
>
> - Why a company would spend billions to launch a product that its own analysts know will fail
> - How a police officer could run right past a brutal assault without seeing it
> - Why award-winning movies are full of editing mistakes
> - What criminals have in common with chess masters
> - Why measles and other childhood diseases are making a comeback
> - Why money managers could learn a lot from weather forecasters

Again and again, we think we experience and understand the world as it is, but our thoughts are beset by everyday illusions. We write traffic laws and build criminal cases on the assumption that people will notice when something unusual happens right in front of them. We're sure we know where we were on 9/11, falsely believing that vivid memories are seared into our mind with perfect fidelity. And as a society, we spend billions on devices to train our brains because we're continually tempted by the lure of quick fixes and effortless self-improvement.

It is easy to bring these ideas into the classroom. There is an excellent National Geographic Channel video series called *Brain Games* that focuses, in part, on the various ways the five senses produce incomplete and misleading information. The Discovery Channel also produces a show entitled *SIGHT—Optical Illusions*. Each issue of *Scientific American Mind* contains a section called "Illusions: Tricks Your Mind Plays on You," which demonstrates how each one of the five senses can produce false impressions.

A common theme of these illusions is the ability of the mind to "fill in" missing information so that our reality appears to be seamless, or whole. The artist Salvador Dali exploited this tendency of our brains to provide the missing pieces so that our conscious minds can see the whole concept. Writing in 2015 for *Scientific American Mind*, Susana Martinez-Conde and Stephen L. Macknik explain as follows:

> In the 1930s Dali developed what he called the panoramic-critical method, which relied on his ability to establish connections between seemingly unrelated concepts of images. In *Paranonia* (1935–1936) a battle scene resembling a Leonardo da Vinci sketch hovers over a silvery, headless female bust, set on a loosely drawn pedestal. Small figures of warriors and horses form parts of the woman's face: eyes, mouth, chin and hairline. Most of her features are absent, but the viewer's visual system fills them in.
>
> Such filling-in processes are common in everyday perception. Face-detecting neurons in the brain's fusiform gyrus area in the temporal lobe are particularly predisposed to detecting the human visage, however

vague or ambiguous. This is why we often see the fronts of cars as faces, with the grills as mouths and the headlights as eyes.

Salvador Dali, *Paranonia*, 1936

A good way to bring this concept into the classroom is to start with sight and hearing, because both of these senses can be represented as waves. As such, they are easily discussed as a spectrum of small-to-large waves. This presents an opportunity to bring science directly into the classroom by way of studying waves.

Sight: Visible light is part of an electromagnetic spectrum of waves ranging from the very large one-thousand-meter long waves to the tiny single-picometer (one trillionth of a meter) gamma rays. Between these two extremes is the wavelength visible to humans, which is a single micron in length, or $1 \times 10{-6}$ of a meter. This wavelength represents just 2.3 percent of the larger electromagnetic spectrum.

Hearing: Sound is measured in cycles per second, or hertz (Hz). Infrasound, sometimes referred to as low-frequency sound, includes sounds under 20 Hz, down to 0.001 Hz. Ultrasound represents high-frequency sound from 20 kHz to 200 MHz and beyond. Sound that is detectable by humans lies between these two extremes, ranging from 20 Hz to 20 kHz, or about 1 percent of the total spectrum of sound.

Smell, touch, and taste: Along with sight and hearing, all five senses can be discussed in terms of the percentage of available data that can be detected by humans. An easy way to demonstrate this in the classroom is to compare what humans can detect to what other animals and machines can detect. In this way, the three senses of smell, touch, and taste can be understood as only a *sampling* of available data. Consequently, we can talk about degrees of sensitivity.

Smell, touch, and taste provide the opportunity to restate the systems-theory dynamic of wholeness. Just as it is essential to make an effort to account for the *whole* of a system, so, too, is it important to be aware that our five senses only provide us with a sample of the whole body of respective data.

A common theme with all five senses is that we tend to think of "sensory input" as a one-way street. In chapter 8, we will discuss various theories of language that break down perception into a series of interconnected processes and will demonstrate how our five senses are just one part of human perception.

Rule # 26
The five human senses of sight, smell, touch, hearing, and taste provide imperfect information about the individual and her or his surrounding environment.

Cognitive Fallibility: While the five human senses provide raw data, that data is processed once it reaches the brain and translated into information. Specifically, sensory data is converted into information through a series of transformations that are so dissimilar that the outcome cannot be equated to dispassionate objectivity. Friedrich Nietzsche was one of the first to recognize that information is nothing but a process. As will be discussed in Chapter 8, Nietzsche understands language as a series of metaphors. We can take Nietzsche's lead and apply what we know about the science of cognition to see it as a series of metaphors:

1. Light hits an object and is reflected outward.
2. Cones and rods of the eye convert this reflected light into neural impulses sent to the brain.
3. The brain converts these impulses into recognizable information.

There is no need to make this discussion complicated, despite the fact that one can pursue an academic career based on this discussion. All that needs to be acknowledged is that cognition is the product of a series of jumps between fundamentally different kinds of data. If the object being observed is a rock, then it is essential we be aware that the human perception of a rock is not the same thing as the rock itself. We "see" the rock as an object independent of our own perception. However, once perception is understood as the linking of dissimilar parts, we can begin to respect not only what we can sense but also what we intellectually understand as the limitations of how the human brain processes the data from our five senses.

The process of cognition becomes fallible when we forget that it is an imperfect tool and begin to believe it as some form of truth. Even though fallibility implies "mistake," it is important that we not blame or label our human processes as solely imperfect, inasmuch as perfection is an idea that lives only in the abstract. The "mistake" is when we begin to believe in the truth of our senses without acknowledging their incomplete nature.

The issue of cognitive fallibility is further complicated by current developments in neuroscience. According to a 2015 article published in the *Proceedings of the National Academy of Sciences,*

> In contrast to canonical, stimulus-driven models of perception, recent proposals argue that perceptual experiences are constructed in an active manner in which top-down influences play a key role. In particular, predictions that the brain makes about the world are incorporated into each perceptual experience. Because forming the appropriate sensory predictions can have a large impact on our visual experiences and visually guided behaviors, a mechanism thought to be disrupted in certain neurological conditions like autism and schizophrenia, an understanding of the neural basis of these predictions is critical. Here, we

provide evidence that perceptual expectations about when a stimulus will appear are instantiated in the brain by optimally configuring pre-stimulus alpha-band oscillations so as to make subsequent processing most efficacious. (Samaha)

The notion that the brain proactively functions in a top-down manner takes the discussion of cognitive fallibility to another level where consciousness is more of a passive than an active act. This article continues by specifically demonstrating how the brain's predictive action can influence perception:

The physiological state of the brain before an incoming stimulus has substantial consequences for subsequent behavior and neural processing. For example, the phase of ongoing posterior alpha-band oscillations (8–14 Hz) immediately before visual stimulation has been shown to predict perceptual outcomes and downstream neural activity. Although this phenomenon suggests that these oscillations may phasically route information through functional networks, many accounts treat these periodic effects as a consequence of ongoing activity that is independent of behavioral strategy...These findings provide direct evidence that forming predictions about when a stimulus will appear can bias the phase of ongoing alpha-band oscillations toward an optimal phase for visual processing, and may thus serve as a mechanism for the top-down control of visual processing guided by temporal predictions.

The upshot of all this for the target audience is that the brain is far more complex than it appears to the naked eye, as our brains themselves influence our perceptions through anticipation.

Rule # 27
Human cognition is a series of imperfect connections between different types of information.

Mnemonic Fallibility: As with cognitive fallibility, mnemonic fallibility is primarily the result of our perception that memory is like a video camera, recording the world around us on a mental tape that we can later replay. It turns out that memories are created from parts and are assembled to form the memory. Each time something is remembered, it is effectively recreated. The problem is that each time a memory is recreated, it can be unconsciously changed—dramatically or subtly. This occurs more often than we might think.

Daniel Schacter discusses the fallible nature of memory in his book *The Seven Sins of Memory: How the Mind Forgets and Remembers*. In it, he classifies the various ways in which memory becomes distorted:

Memory Sins by Omission

1. Transience: Loss of memory over time
2. Absentmindedness: Breakdown in the relationship between attention and memory
3. Blocking: Inability to access a memory

Memory Sins by Commission

4. Misattribution: Assigning a memory to the wrong source
5. Suggestibility: Implanted memories resulting from leading questions, comments, or suggestions
6. Bias: The influences of our current knowledge and beliefs on how we remember our past
7. Persistence: Repeated recall of disturbing information or events that we would prefer to banish from our minds altogether

Keep in mind that the education objective here is not to have students memorize these seven classifications for Friday's test, which will then be forgotten by the following Monday. The point is for students to understand and respect that memory is not the product of an objective digital recording. Memory is an imperfect tool that is prone to error and should be used with great caution.

Since self-identity is partly based on memory, teachers can take the opportunity to say a few words about how a deeper understanding of memory can facilitate a deeper understanding of the self. We normally think of ourselves as a product of our past, so that memory is directly tied to self-identity and self-knowledge. A memory that creeps into our day may seem like a digital image of the past but is, in fact, a mirage created by both conscious and unconscious influences. If we believe these memories and allow our mind to play endless reruns, it can lead to personal delusion and even mental illness.

Rule # 28
Memories must be held suspect and independently confirmed before they can be relied upon as the basis of evidence.

Social Fallibility: The purpose of this section is to look at humanity as falling into one of two camps: those with a healthy sense of empathy and those without. Those with an organic inability to experience empathy are labeled psychopaths. While this line of empathetic demarcation is simplistic, the larger discussion of classification and diagnosis is more complicated. To keep it simple, the Game considers a lack of empathy as a form of social fallibility, particularly when the majority with empathy forgets there is a minority that lacks it.

Given the skill of psychopaths at hiding their nature, our failure to remember this reality is understandable. The first book a layperson should read on this topic is Hervey Cleckley's seminal text *The Mask of Sanity*, which, for the first time, brought the term "psychopath" into popular usage. First published in 1941 and revised five times throughout his academic career, the text has now been made available for free by his family. *The Mask of Sanity* is an enthralling read, as Cleckley presents case studies to demonstrate his clinical theories. By the time you finish the book, you will see the nuance and complexity of the psychopathic mind in a way that is often missed by reading a dry academic text.

The study of psychopathy is complicated because of the masking quality identified by Cleckley: the ability of the psychopath to access the appearance of empathy at will. While there have been studies conducted on incarcerated psychopaths, nothing similar has been carried out with "successful" psychopaths who have integrated themselves into society. After all, how do you identify a group of people for study when they have the ability and predisposition to hide?

Since Cleckley brought the term *psychopathy* into the mainstream, others have conducted considerable work on the topic. Terminology has evolved to include sociopathology, and the *Diagnostic and Statistical Manual of Mental Disorders* (DSM) and *International Classification of Diseases* (ICD) have introduced the diagnoses of antisocial-personality disorder (ASPD) and disso-cial personality disorder as extensions of psychopathy or sociopathy.

The National Institute of Mental Health (NIMH) follows the fourth edition of the American Psychiatric Association's *Diagnostic and Statistical Manual on Mental Disorders* (DSM-IV) to define ASPD as "a pervasive pattern of disregard for, and violation of, the rights of others that begins in childhood or early adolescence and continues into adulthood." The NIH goes on to describe how "people with antisocial personality disorder may disregard social norms and laws, repeatedly lie, place others at risk for their own benefit, and demonstrate a profound lack of remorse. It is sometimes referred to as sociopathic personality disorder, or sociopathy."

However, there is an academically identified upside to those who lack empathy. The Stanford Graduate School of Business writes the following:

> Successful investors in the stock market might plausibly be called "functional psychopaths." These individuals are either much better at controlling their emotions, or perhaps don't experience emotions with the same intensity as others do. "Many CEOs and many top lawyers might also share this trait," said Baba Shiv, professor of marketing at Stanford GSB and coauthor of the study, *Investment Behavior and the Negative Side of Emotion*. "Being less emotional can help you in certain situations."

For some, it appears that having empathy is just a burden that gets in the way of making money.

Are individuals born sociopaths, or is it a lifestyle choice? Martha Stout, who served on the clinical faculty of the Harvard Medical School for over twenty-five years, addresses this nature-versus-nurture question in her book, *The Sociopath Next Door*. According to Stout,

> There is credible evidence that some cultures contain fewer sociopaths than do other cultures. Disturbingly, the prevalence of sociopathy in the United States seems to be increasing. The 1991 Epidemiologic Catchment Area study, sponsored by the National Institute of Mental Health, reported that in the fifteen years preceding the study, the prevalence of

antisocial personality disorder had nearly doubled among the young in America. It would be difficult, closing in on impossible, to explain such a dramatically rapid shift in terms of genetics or neurobiology.

The notion that an individual's empathy can be influenced by environment is supported by numerous studies. Writing in 2013 for Psychology Today, Wharton professor Adam Grant provides an overview of these studies and concludes

- In the US, economics professors gave less money to charity than professors in other fields
- Economics students in Germany were more likely than students from other majors to recommend an overpriced plumber when they were paid to do it.
- Economics majors and students who had taken at least three economics courses were more likely than their peers to rate greed as "generally good," "correct," and "moral."
- Students were given $10 and had to make a proposal about how to divide the money with a peer. If the peer accepted, they had a deal, but if the peer declined, both sides got nothing. On average, economics students proposed to keep 13% more money for themselves than students from other majors.

Grant goes on to question whether these results are evidence of a predisposed selfish nature or an indication that studying economics can shift people towards selfishness. According to Grant's review of the literature,

- Altruistic Values Drop Among Economics Majors
- Economics Students Stay Selfish, Even Though Their Peers Become More Cooperative
- After Taking Economics, Students Become More Selfish and Expect Worse of Others
- Just Thinking about Economics Can Make Us Less Caring

This last point, how just thinking about economics can result in lowered empathy, is based on Grant's own research, which he describes as

Exposure to economic words might be enough to inhibit compassion and concern for others, even among experienced executives. In one experiment, Andy Molinsky, Joshua Margolis, and I recruited presidents, CEOs, partners, VPs, directors, and managers who supervised an average of 140 employees. We randomly assigned them to unscramble 30 sentences, with either neutral phrases like [green tree was a] or economic words like [continues economy growing our].

Then, the executives wrote letters conveying bad news to an employee who was transferred to an undesirable city and disciplining a highly competent employee for being late to meetings because she lacked a car. Independent coders rated their letters for compassion.

Executives who unscrambled sentences with economic words expressed significantly less compassion. There were two factors at play: empathy and unprofessionalism. After thinking about economics, executives felt less empathy—and even when they did empathize, they worried that expressing concern and offering help would be inappropriate.

It is clear that for many, empathy is a malleable state of mind that can be influenced by one's environment. It is due to this nature of empathy that the game provides Empathy Maintenance Tools (chapter 7) to ensure an individual's empathy is cultivated and remains healthy.

To argue that an individual's empathy is not cultivated and otherwise in a state of unhealthy disrepair is not the same thing as a clinical diagnosis. A clinical diagnosis of ASPD requires numerous markers in a person's early years and on through adulthood to evidence a behavioral basis for ASPD. But what about the person who grew up displaying normal behaviors only to become an adult banker or politician? Did Lloyd Craig Blankfein, chief executive officer and chairman of Goldman Sachs, torture small animals or otherwise demonstrate antisocial behavior as a small child? Does it matter when the adult outcome is the same?

I can personally attest to the social fallibility of Wall Street that encourages people to brag about lying, cheating, or otherwise defrauding customers. To brag in this way is thought to demonstrate one's personal power and cleverness.

In effect, if someone doesn't represent his or her efforts as predatory, he or she is seen by fellow workers and bosses as being weak and unmotivated. I tried making such boasts, but I always felt that I was a fraud for doing so. Eventually, burdened by the inconvenience of empathy, I quit the industry. With all the money, power, and family support that often accompany a successful securities career, it is understandable how some might be drawn into the psychopathic lifestyle.

The pitfall here, however, is that just because someone acts selfishly and without apparent remorse, it doesn't mean that person is clinically a sociopath; he or she may just be a selfish person with what the Game refers to as "lazy" empathy. In other words, the capacity for empathy exists, but as the person has spent a lifetime repressing that capacity, it has atrophied.

The problem with sociopaths is that they do not share with the rest of us a desire to act in good faith. The manipulation of language is one of the means by which psychopaths get what they want. As such, a psychopath is free to use language without any concern for how that use relates to the physical world and how the resulting impact of language manipulation can affect others and the greater socioeconomic system.

Psychopathy becomes a social fallibility when its place in society is forgotten. Those of us with a healthy sense of empathy are not preconditioned to expect others to differ in this regard. We simply assume that everyone else is like us. We then take this assumption and proceed to use language as if we are all the same.

Robert D. Hare is a researcher in the field of criminal psychology and the author of the Hare Psychopathy Checklist, a psychological-assessment tool used to identify the presence of psychopathy in individuals. High scores are associated with impulsivity, aggression, Machiavellianism, and persistent criminal behavior—all of which are associated with a lack of empathy. Today, Hare's list has been revised and is now known as the Psychopathy Checklist—revised (PCL-R) that combines Hare's work with that of Mask of Sanity author, Hervey M. Cleckley.

Psychopathy Checklist—revised (PCL-R):
Emotional/Interpersonal:

- Glib and superficial
- Egocentric and grandiose
- Lack of remorse or guilt
- Lack of empathy
- Deceitful and manipulative
- Shallow emotions

Social Deviance:

- Impulsive
- Poor behavior controls
- Need for excitement
- Lack of responsibility
- Early behavior problems
- Adult antisocial behavior (Skeem)

Hare writes that he believes "our society is moving in the direction of permitting, reinforcing, and in some instances actually valuing some of the traits listed in the Psychopathy Checklist—traits such as impulsivity, irresponsibility, lack of remorse."

In their book, *Snakes in Suits: When Psychopaths Go to Work*, Hare and his coauthor Paul Babiak estimate that while psychopaths represent about 1 percent of the general population, they occupy 3–4 percent of senior positions in business. This concentration of psychopaths in business has generated an entire sector of academic study referred to as "Psychopathy in the Workplace." Academics have coined labels, such as executive psychopaths, corporate psychopaths, business psychopaths, successful psychopaths, office psychopaths, white-collar psychopaths, industrial psychopaths, organizational psychopaths, and occupational psychopaths.

The problem with psychopaths in the workplace is the way they undermine the assumption that everyone within the group works from a place of good faith. Specifically, psychopaths undermine the assumption that an organization is unified around a common mission statement. When an organization is allowed to become untethered from the constraints of its mission statement, the resulting detrimental effects include increased bullying, conflict, stress, staff turnover, and absenteeism as well as reductions in productivity and social responsibility.

ASPD becomes a fallibility when those of us with a healthy sense of empathy forget that there are those among us who have a deficient or nonexistent degree of empathy, the capacity to understand or feel what another person is experiencing from within the other person's frame of reference. The student takeaway is that while most of us enjoy a healthy sense of empathy, a small minority lacks such a capacity and is otherwise driven to positions of power.

Rule # 29
Those humans lacking the ability to experience empathy are disproportionately drawn to positions of power.

Interpersonal Fallibility: A common question about the nature of humanity is whether or not humans are driven by rational thought. Self-deception is the process of rejecting rational thought by denying or rationalizing away the relevance, significance, or importance of opposing evidence and logical arguments. Self-deception involves so completely convincing oneself of a truth (or lack of truth) that one does not recognize the deception. Another way of looking at self-deception is that it is structurally opposed to good-faith actions because good-faith actions imply an honest relationship with physical evidence.

Self-deception and its place in groupthink is a primary theme of Mark Twain's last novel, The Mysterious Stranger. In a conversation between the story's main characters, 2-boys named Theodor and Satan, Satan discusses the role self-denial plays in a nation's psychological buildup to war

> The pulpit will-- warily and cautiously--object--at first; the great, big, dull bulk of the nation will rub its sleepy eyes and try to make out why there should be a war, and will say, earnestly and indignantly, "It is unjust and dishonorable, and there is no necessity for it." Then the handful will shout louder. A few fair men on the other side will argue and reason against the war with speech and pen, and at first will have a hearing and be applauded; but it will not last long; those others will outshout them, and presently the anti-war audiences will thin out and lose popularity. Before long you will see this curious thing: the

speakers stoned from the platform, and free speech strangled by hordes of furious men who in their secret hearts are still at one with those stoned speakers--as earlier-- but do not dare to say so. And now the whole nation--pulpit and all-- will take up the war-cry, and shout itself hoarse, and mob any honest man who ventures to open his mouth; and presently such mouths will cease to open. Next the statesmen will invent cheap lies, putting the blame upon the nation that is attacked, and every man will be glad of those conscience-soothing falsities, and will diligently study them, and refuse to examine any refutations of them; and thus he will by and by convince himself that the war is just, and will thank God for the better sleep he enjoys after this process of grotesque self-deception."

Self-deception becomes a fallibility when we forget the propensity of human nature for irrationality and decision making without regard for relevant evidence. Like a drug, self-denial gives people the feeling they want. A by-product of self-deception is what American social psychologist Leon Festinger (1957) calls "cognitive dissonance," the mental stress or discomfort experienced by an individual who holds two or more contradictory beliefs, ideas, or values at the same time.

Rule # 30
The unconscious mind is skilled and motivated to deceive the individual.

Human Needs

Every human shares the same core group of needs. Abraham Maslow was an American psychologist who was best known for creating his hierarchy of needs. In his 1943 paper "A Theory of Human Motivation," Maslow used the following terms to describe the steps that human motivations generally pass through:

- Physiological needs
- Safety needs
- Love and belonging

- Self-esteem
- Self-actualization
- Self-transcendence

What sets Maslow's work apart from other investigations of the human mind is that he studied healthy people rather than mentally ill or neurotic individuals.

Rule # 31
The Human Operator of language is influenced by the five basic human needs: psychological health, safety, belonging, self-esteem, and self-actualization.

Human Emotions

Paul Ekman is an American psychologist and pioneer in the study of emotions and their relation to facial expressions. Ekman's work supports the view that emotions are discrete, measurable, and physiologically distinct. His most influential work revolves around the finding that certain emotions appear to be universally recognized. His research findings have led him to classify the six basic human emotions as

- Fear,
- Love,
- Joy,
- Surprise,
- Anger, and
- Sadness.

Certainly, this is not a perfect list, and one or more players of the Game may wish to argue that this list should be expanded or contracted. The larger point is that all humans are motivated by a set of underlying emotions that are so prevalent that we don't realize the extent of their control or influence over our interpretations of reality. Take any one of the above terms and think back on a time in your own life when this emotion took over your otherwise-rational thinking and produced an unexpected, and probably undesirable, outcome. If you need examples of human weakness from which to work, simply turn on an episode of *Judge Judy* or *Jerry Springer* for inspiration.

The point is that when human language operators use language without understanding how basic human emotions can influence perceptions of reality, both information flow and the capacity for empathy are disrupted. It is impossible to care about something for which you are ignorant.

Rule # 32
The Human Operator of language is influenced by the six basic human emotions: fear, love, joy, surprise, anger, and sadness.

Human Wounds

Mario Martinez is a licensed clinical psychologist and best-selling author of *The Mind-Body Code: How to Change the Beliefs that Limit Your Health, Longevity, and Success*. Martinez invites readers to discover the dynamic interplay between their thoughts, body, and cultural history. According to Martinez, "All cultures, East and West, have their own unique ways of punishing those whose ideas and behaviors run contrary to established beliefs." These strategies get transmitted from parents to children and show up in our relationships when we fall in love. As a result, "these forms of punishment cause emotional damage that surface in the form of three archetypal wounds," which Martinez describes as the following:

- Abandonment
- Shame
- Betrayal

Rule # 33
The Human Operator of language is influenced by the three basic human wounds: abandonment, shame, and betrayal.

Human Weaknesses

Western religion addresses human weakness as *sin*. However, in the context of the Game, human weakness is not about sin, as that would be a metaphysical approach to understanding the human condition. Rather, the issue of human weakness is approached from the perspective of the Golden Rule that directs us to do unto others as we wish to be done unto us.

Dante's *Inferno* is used to understand the timeless nature of these human emotions through studying the seven deadly sins. It is in this context that questions are asked, such as "Why are humans so quick to broadly condemn the poor as lazy yet less quick to broadly condemn the wealthy as greedy?"

The Game represents the following as imbalanced states of being:

The Seven Deadly Sins

Lust (Latin, *luxuria*) (fornication, perversion): Lust is described as depraved thought, unwholesome morality, the desire for excitement, or the need to be accepted or recognized by others. Notice how this standard church-based definition identifies the unbalanced nature of thought or act. It is not lustful to allow your thoughts to wander all over the spectrum, but it is lustful when thoughts become dominated by obsessive, unlawful, or unnatural sexual desires, such as desiring sex with a person outside of marriage or engaging in unnatural sexual appetites (like bestiality). Rape, adultery, and sodomy are considered to be extreme forms of lust and mortal sins. The punishment in hell for lust is being smothered in fire and brimstone.

Gluttony (Latin, *gula)* (waste, overindulgence): Gluttony is described as the thoughtless waste of everything, overindulgence, misplaced sensuality, uncleanliness, and the malicious deprivation of others. It is marked by a refusal to share and the unreasonable consumption of more than is necessary, especially in the case of food or water; destruction, especially for sport (like trophy hunting); and substance abuse or binge drinking. The punishment in hell for gluttony is being force-fed rats, toads, and snakes.

Greed/avarice (Latin, *avaritia)* (treachery, covetousness): Greed is described as a strong desire for gain, especially in terms of money or power. It is characterized by disloyalty, deliberate betrayal, or treason, especially for personal gain or compensation; scavenging and hoarding of materials or objects; and theft and robbery, especially by violence, trickery, or, worst of all, manipulation of authority. Greed is often seen as the most childish of the three exaggerated adulthood sins because it often focuses only on short-term gains. It is an extreme form of gluttony. Greed is represented by the frog and the color yellow. The punishment in hell for greed is being submerged in the finest boiling oils.

Sloth/laziness (Latin, *acedia)* (apathy, indifference): Sloth is described as apathy, idleness, and wastefulness of time. Laziness is particularly condemned because others must work harder to make up for it. It is characterized by cowardice or irresponsibility, and abandonment, especially of God. Sloth is a little like a state of equilibrium: one does not produce much; one does not consume much. However, sloth, unlike homeostasis, leads only to despair. Associated with goats and the color light blue, the punishment in hell for sloth is being thrown into a pit of snakes.

Wrath (Latin, *ira)* (anger, hatred, prejudice, discrimination): Wrath is described as inappropriate (unrighteous) feelings of hatred and anger. It is characterized by the denial of truth to others or the self; impatience with the law or seeking revenge outside of justice; unnecessary vigilantism; the wish to do evil or harm to others; the dislike of others for no good reason, such as their race or religion, that leads to discrimination; and self-righteousness. Wrath is the root of murder, assault, discrimination, and, ultimately, genocide. Wrath is symbolized by the bear and the color red. The punishment in hell for wrath is being dismembered (probably over and over again, like how the eagle repeatedly eats Prometheus' liver every day in Greek mythology.)

Envy (Latin, *invidia*) (jealousy, malice): Envy is described as spite and resentment over the material objects, accomplishments, or character traits of others, or wishing others to fail or come to harm. Envy is the root of theft and self-loathing. It is associated with the dog and the color green, and it is the adolescent of the three exaggerated adulthood sins. The punishment in hell for envy is being placed in freezing water.

Pride (Latin, *superbia*) (vanity, narcissism): Pride is known as the father of all sins. Pride is characterized by a desire to be more important or attractive to others, the failure to give credit to others, or the excessive love of self (especially with respect to God). Pride was what sparked the fall of Lucifer from Heaven and his subsequent transformation into Satan. Vanity and narcissism are good examples of this type of sin. They often lead to the destruction of the sinner, for instance through the wanton squandering of money and time on themselves without caring about others, as in the Greek tale of Echo and Narcissus. Pride can be seen as the misplacement of morals. Associated with the horse, the lion, the peacock, and the color violet, the punishment in hell for pride is being broken on the wheel.

Rule # 34
The Human Operator is influenced by the seven basic human weaknesses: lust, gluttony, greed, sloth, wrath, envy, and pride.

Chapter Bibliography

Babiak, Paul, and Robert D. Hare. 2006. *Snakes in Suits: When Psychopaths Go to Work*. New York: HarperCollins. 27

Chabris, Christopher, and Daniel Simons. 2010. *The Invisible Gorilla and Other Ways Our Intuitions Deceive Us*. New York: Harmony.

Chabris, Christopher, and Daniel Simons. 2010a. "The Invisible Gorilla" (videos). http://www.theinvisiblegorilla.com/videos.html

Cleckley, Hervey. 1988. *The Mask of Sanity: An Attempt to Clarify Some Issues About the So-Called Psychopathic Personality.* Fifth Edition: private printing for non-profit educational use: http://cassiopaea.org/cass/sanity_1.PdF

Dali, Salvador. *Paranonia*, 1935-36 oil on canvas. ©Salvador Dali, Fundacio Gala-Salvador Dali, (Artist Rights Society), 2016. Collection of the Salvador Dali Museum, Inc., St. Petersburg, FL (USA) 2016. ©2016 Salvador Dali Museum, Inc.

Ekman, Paul. 1999. "Basic Emotions." In *Handbook of Cognition and Emotion.* Edited by T. Dalgleish and M. Power, 45–60. Sussex, UK: John Wiley & Sons.

Festinger, Leon. 1957. *A Theory of Cognitive Dissonance.* Stanford, CA: Stanford University Press.

Grant, Adam. *Does Studying Economics Breed Greed? Even thinking about economics can make us less compassionate.* Psychology Today, Oct 22, 2013. https://www.psychologytoday.com/blog/give-and-take/201310/does-studying-economics-breed-greed

Hare, Robert D. 2003. *Manual for the Revised Psychopathy Checklist.* Toronto: Multi-Health Systems. 92

Kihlstrom, John F. 1992. "The Psychological Unconscious: Found, Lost, and Regained." *The American Psychologist* 47 (6): 788–91.

Martinez, Mario. 2009. *The Mind-Body Code: How the Mind Wounds and Heals the Body.* Louisville, CO: Sounds True. 27, 62.

Martinez-Conde, Susana, and Stephen L. Macknik. 2015. "Dali's Doubles." *Scientific American Mind* 26: 20–1.

Maslow, Abraham. 1943. "A Theory of Human Motivation." *Psychological Review* 50 (4): 370–96. https://docs.google.com/file/d/0B-5-JeCa2Z7hN-jZlNDNhOTEtMWNkYi00YmFhLWI3YjUtMDEyMDJkZDExNWRm/edit#!

National Institute of Mental Health. n.d. "Antisocial Personality Disorder." http://www.nimh.nih.gov/health/statistics/prevalence/antisocial-personality-disorder.shtml

Samaha, Jason, Phoebe Bauer, Sawyer Cimaroli, and Bradley R. Postle. 2015. "Top-Down Control of the Phase of Alpha-Band Oscillations as a Mechanism for Temporal Prediction." *Proceedings of the National Academy of Sciences* 112 (27): 8439–44. doi:10.1073/pnas.1503686112. http://www.pnas.org/content/112/27/8439.full?sid=e5f990bc-2ae0-4167-ba8f-56ac09051af6

Schacter, Daniel. 2001. *The Seven Sins of Memory: How the Mind Forgets and Remembers.* Boston: Houghton Mifflin. 132

Skeem, J. L.; Polaschek, D. L. L.; Patrick, C. J.; Lilienfeld, S. O. (2011). "Psychopathic Personality: Bridging the Gap Between Scientific Evidence and Public Policy". Psychological Science in the Public Interest 12 (3): 95–162. http://www.psychologicalscience.org/index.php/publications/journals/pspi/psychopathy.html

Stanford Graduate School of Business Staff. 2005. "Baba Shiv: Emotions Can Negatively Impact Investment Decisions." *Insights by Stanford Business,* September 1. https://www.gsb.stanford.edu/insights/baba-shiv-emotions-can-negatively-impact-investment-decisions

Stout, Martha. 2005. *The Sociopath Next Door.* New York: Harmony. 132

Twain, Mark. 1908 *The Mysterious Stranger.* University of California Press (1982) http://www.classicreader.com/book/1370/9/

CHAPTER 7
System Rules

> In today's regulatory environment, it's
> virtually impossible to violate rules.
> BERNIE MADOFF

The previous chapter on human nature provided clear evidence on how our nature can cause imbalance in the way we use language. The goal of the Game is to design a system that is focused on using language to represent the physical world. But, how do we create a process that ensures the Operator of language does not derail the Operation of language in its quest to represent the physical world? The answer is to craft a procedural buffer between language and human nature through the use of evidence-based rules. Rather than being altruistic, this approach to rules is in line with the stated objectives of the system.

Since the Game is organized around systems theory, we seek to discover processes rather than metaphysically based rules sent down from on high. The pervasive nature of the Golden Rule throughout history suggests it is born of observing human nature:

> **Confucianism**: "Do not do to others what you would not like yourself. Then there will be no resentment against you, either in the family or in the state."
> ANALECTS 12:2

> **Buddhism**: "Hurt not others in ways that you yourself would find hurtful."
> UDANA-VARGA 5:1

Christianity: "All things whatsoever ye would that men should do to you, do ye so to them; for this is the law and the prophets."
MATTHEW 7:1

Hinduism: "This is the sum of duty; do naught unto others what you would not have them do unto you."
MAHABHARATA 5: 1517

Islam: "No one of you is a believer until he desires for his brother that which he desires for himself."
FORTY HADITH OF AN-NAWAWI 13

Judaism: "What is hateful to you, do not do to your fellowman. This is the entire Law; all the rest is commentary."
TALMUD, SHABBAT 31D

Taoism: "Regard your neighbor's gain as your gain, and your neighbor's loss as your own loss."
TAI SHANG KAN YING P'IEN

Zoroastrianism: "That nature alone is good which refrains from doing another whatsoever is not good for itself."
DADISTEN-I-DINIK 94:5

As the above quotes demonstrate, civilization has been preaching the Golden Rule at least since the beginning of human history. Yet, rather than the world falling into benevolent order, we are still dropping bombs on people and otherwise displacing millions from their homes and lives through war. From the Game's perspective, the reason the Golden Rule has failed to produce widespread benevolence is because it has been taught as a religious top-down ideal rather than as a process.

The answer to our quest for an evidence-based buffer between the Operation and Operator of language is the Golden Rule, which describes a reciprocal, or two-way, relationship between one's self and others that involves both sides equally. Rather than a "Thou-shalt" form of morality, the Golden Rule is a process with a built-in mechanism that makes it all but impervious to the very human shenanigans we are trying to mitigate.

One thing that the human mind is very adept at is weaseling its way out of taking responsibility for something by rationalizing its behavior. Sure, it's a good idea to love your neighbor, but right now I need to exploit my neighbor because of X, Y, and Z. And, besides, my neighbor is not like me. By making our interactions with our neighbors about how we want to be treated, the Golden Rule denies the possibility of exception and otherwise creates a perfect process for combating selfish rationalizations.

There is no act that cannot be informed by the Golden Rule. For instance, consider "Bomb your neighbor as you wish to be bombed." Today, it is US foreign policy to drop bombs on people in distant countries without declaring war or conducting meaningful due process. Is the deployment of bombs how we want other nations to treat us if they don't like what we are doing on the international stage? Given our response to the 9/11 attacks, apparently not.

One of the best ways to justify ignoring the Golden Rule is to consider your adversary to be less than human and, therefore, not covered by the Golden Rule. Consider how the following two views differ on the problem of rape in the military.

Radio host Michael Savage said about hearings related to sexual assault in the US military, "I watch these Khmer Rouge feminists try to take over the military, this looked like an attempted coup to me...I know most of the sexual assault cases are invented, I know it for a fact...'Oh, I didn't want to go on a date with him, I feel threatened, I feel uncomfortable.' They're now calling that sexual assault." (Hananoki)

In contrast, Lieutenant General David Morrison, Australian chief of army, said, "Those who think that it is OK to behave in a way that demeans or exploits their colleagues have *no* place in this army...Female soldiers and officers have proven themselves worthy of the best traditions of the Australian Army...If that does not suit you, then *get out*...The standard you walk past is the standard you accept." (Barber)

119

Notice how the first quote focuses on lawless women lying and otherwise being overly dramatic about their claim of rape. The Khmer Rouge was a genocidal political organization responsible for over a million deaths. In associating rape victims with mass murder, Savage is making an *ad hominem* attack, asserting that "these women" are not worthy of our concern and, therefore, not eligible for coverage under the Golden Rule. To him, they are less than human.

By contrast, notice how Morrison focuses on the humanity of women. Morrison's perspective serves his organization by the way it demands integrity from all. There is even an echo of the Golden Rule in his comment that "The standard you walk past is the standard you accept." Which of these two speakers represents a stronger form of human system?

The Golden Rule is not a panacea for what ails humanity. As with self-knowledge, it is not a thing but a process. And, like any process, there must be a good-faith effort behind it for the process to produce the desired results. Again, the discussion comes back to systems theory and the role of the integrity between principles and action. Take, for example, the scientific fraud described in chapter 3. Examples of fraudulent science abound. In each case, the governing processes have not been operated with integrity. Processes are only as good as the intention of the operator. This is true of any system, be it language, science, or the law.

A 2012 study by Fang, Steen, and Casadevall concluded that the proportion of scientific research retracted due to fraud has increased tenfold since 1975. Expanding on this theme, the *New York Times* reported,

> A scientific journal has retracted sixty papers linked to a researcher in Taiwan, accusing him of "perverting the peer-review process" by creating fraudulent online accounts to judge the papers favorably and help get them published.
>
> Sage Publications, publisher of *The Journal of Vibration and Control*, in which the papers appeared over the last four years, said the researcher, Chen-Yuan Chen, had established a "peer-review and citation ring" consisting of fake scientists as well as real ones whose identities he had

assumed. It said that in at least one case, Mr. Chen, who also uses the first name Peter, reviewed his own paper using one of the aliases.

In all, Mr. Chen, an associate professor of computer science who resigned in February from the National Pingtung University of Education amid an investigation, appears to have created 130 e-mail accounts that were used in reviewing the papers. A spokeswoman for the publisher said it had contacted all the accounts but received no replies. (Fountain)

Then there is, in my estimation, the crowning jewel of scientific fraud where bad faith meets technology. According to an article in the science journal *Nature*,

The publishers Springer and IEEE are removing more than 120 papers from their subscription services after a French researcher discovered that the works were computer-generated nonsense.

Over the past two years, computer scientist Cyril Labbé of Joseph Fourier University in Grenoble, France, has catalogued computer-generated papers that made it into more than thirty published conference proceedings between 2008 and 2013. Sixteen appeared in publications by Springer, which is headquartered in Heidelberg, Germany, and more than one hundred were published by the Institute of Electrical and Electronic Engineers (IEEE), based in New York. Both publishers, which were privately informed by Labbé, say that they are now removing the papers.

Among the works were, for example, a paper published as a proceeding from the 2013 International Conference on Quality, Reliability, Risk, Maintenance, and Safety Engineering, held in Chengdu, China. (The conference website says that all manuscripts are "reviewed for merits and contents.") The authors of the paper, entitled "TIC: a methodology for the construction of e-commerce," write in the abstract that they "concentrate our efforts on disproving that spreadsheets can be made knowledge-based, empathic, and compact." (Van Noorden)

Rule # 35
The Golden Rule is the basis of all Game Rules and the primary tool for ensuring integrity and balance between the human Operator and the linguistic Operation of language.

It is one thing to laud the capacities of the Golden Rule and quite another to see it in action. How can society ensure the use of the Golden Rule as an ongoing practice? The underlying engine of the Golden Rule is empathy. So another way of asking the same question is how does society foster empathy? Since empathy is a state of mind, the Game addresses this issue with three Empathy-maintenance Tools:

- Compassion
- Forgiveness
- Redemption

Practicing compassion and forgiveness and believing in the inherent capacity for redemption are all part of empathy. Furthermore, these three acts are as equally valuable for relating to others as they are for relating to the self. So, again, we return to self-knowledge and its relationship to enlightenment. To practice empathy toward others is the same as practicing empathy toward ourselves. We always need to be reminded of the importance of forgiving ourselves and believing in our capacity for improvement. We first have to have our own house in order before we are able to go out and understand others.

Notice how these Empathy-maintenance Tools relate to the seven human weaknesses (seven deadly sins). Specifically, look at the power of greed as a contraindicator of the Golden Rule. A study by Paul K. Piff, entitled "Higher Social Class Predicts Increased Unethical Behavior," found,

> Seven studies using experimental and naturalistic methods reveal that upper-class individuals behave more unethically than lower-class individuals. In studies one and two, upper-class individuals were more likely to break the law while driving, relative to lower-class individuals. In follow-up laboratory studies, upper-class individuals were more likely to exhibit unethical decision-making tendencies (study three),

take valued goods from others (study four), lie in a negotiation (study five), cheat to increase their chances of winning a prize (study six), and endorse unethical behavior at work (study seven) than were lower-class individuals. Mediator and moderator data demonstrated that upper-class individuals' unethical tendencies are accounted for, in part, by their more favorable attitudes toward greed.

There is a link between the Rules as laid out above and increased awareness. Empathy is a process that nurtures healthy interactions within systems and within the individuals who populate such systems.

Rule # 36
The Game requires players to proactively maintain healthy empathy toward others through the maintenance of the tools of compassion, forgiveness, and redemption.

Chapter Bibliography

Fang, Ferric C., R. Grant Steen, and Arturo Casadevall. 2012. "Misconduct Accounts for the Majority of Retracted Scientific Publications." *Proceedings of the National Academy of Sciences* 109 (42): 17028–33. doi:10.1073/pnas.1212247109. http://www.pnas.org/content/109/42/17028. full?sid=60305bbf-2010-4234-88b2-b6a589fdb2a8

Fountain, Henry. 2014. "Science Journal Pulls Sixty Papers in Peer-Review Fraud." *The New York Times*, July 10. http://www.nytimes.com/2014/07/11/ science/science-journal-pulls-60-papers-in-peer-review-fraud.html?_r=0

Barber, Cam. *David Morrison Speech Transcript: The standard you walk past is the standard you accept.* August 13, 2013. CamBarber, The Message Man. http:// vividmethod.com/transcript-the-standard-you-walk-past-is-the-standard-you-accept/

Piff, Paul K. 2008. "Higher Social Class Predicts Increased Unethical Behavior." *Proceedings of the National Academy of Sciences* 109 (11): 4086–91. doi: 10.1073/pnas.1118373109. http://www.pnas.org/content/109/11/4086.full?sid=b6338259-d5bf-4c0d-b0d7-def53fe631e9

Hananoki, Eric. *Fox's Allen West Uses Military Sexual Assault Epidemic To Attack Democrats And Decry Women In Combat Units.* Media Matters for America, June 6, 2013. http://mediamatters.org/blog/2013/06/06/foxs-allen-west-uses-military-sexual-assault-ep/194378

Van Noorden, Richard. 2014. "Publishers Withdraw More Than 120 Gibberish Papers." *Nature*, September 24. http://www.nature.com/news/publishers-withdraw-more-than-120-gibberish-papers-1.14763

CHAPTER 8
Language Theory

The limits of my language mean the limits of my world.

LUDWIG WITTGENSTEIN,
TRACTATUS LOGICO-PHILOSOPHICUS

Every student of the English language should have a basic understanding of language-theory history. This is important not only because the present is a product of the past, but also because it is essential for everyone to have a sense of ownership of this history for the sake of intellectual confidence and the continued development of understanding.

My strategy is not to introduce this history as a fixed timeline of ideas, names, and dates but to build a narrative around a theme. In this study, the theme is to ask the question: what is the relationship between language and the quest for truth where change is constant?

Crafting such a history is difficult on a number of fronts. There is the problem of oral tradition and the lost transcripts from the early days of writing. Even in cases where there are written records, it is problematic to say that a specific statement best characterizes a particular philosopher. In 1932, Arthur O. Lovejoy gave a series of lectures at Harvard, which were later turned into the book *The Great Chain of Being*. In his lectures, Lovejoy laid out an overview of Western philosophy and introduced his analysis by saying

> The total body of doctrine of any philosopher or school is almost always a complex and heterogeneous aggregate—and often in ways the philosopher himself does not suspect. It is not only a compound but an

unstable compound, though, age after age, each new philosopher usually forgets this melancholy truth…When the student reviews the vast sequence of arguments and opinions that fill our historical textbooks, he is likely to feel bewildered by the multiplicity and seeming diversity of the matters presented. Even if the array of material is simplified somewhat by the aid of conventional—and largely misleading—classifications of philosophers by schools or -isms, it still appears extremely various and complicated; each age seems to evolve new species of reasoning and conclusions, even upon the same old problems…I do not, of course, mean to maintain that essentially novel conceptions, new problems and new modes of reasoning about them, do not from time to time emerge in the history of thought. But such increments of absolute novelty seem to me a good deal rarer than is sometimes supposed.

From the perspective of a student, there is the additional problem of adulation towards the historical figure, text, or idea. Education should be about thought and not about worship, which is the absence of thought. So, it is essential to set the stage for discussing these ideas so that students can see that the historical trajectory is a "complex and heterogeneous aggregate" of ideas and not an objective timeline to be memorized for an exam.

What is the nature of truth? Is truth universal or does it change according to the time and place? How can we tell? For the Greeks, the answer to this question revolved around whether or not change was constant or nonexistent.

Heraclitus (535–475 BCE): Change Is Constant

Heraclitus is the pre-Socratic patron of the Game, not least because he is known for asserting that change is constant. Plato's dialogue "Cratylus" is a conversation between Socrates, Cratylus, a disciple of Heraclitus, and another. Twice during the dialogue, Heraclitus is associated with change:

- "Heraclitus is supposed to say that all things are in motion and nothing at rest; he compares them to the stream of a river, and says that you cannot go into the same water twice."

- "Those again who read *osia* seem to have inclined to the opinion of Heraclitus, that all things flow and nothing stands."

Here, Heraclitus observes that we know change is constant because we can perceive this change through our five senses.

Parmenides (515–460 BCE): There Is No Change

Heraclitus was not the only major pre-Socratic Greek philosopher who was interested in change. Parmenides, a contemporary of Heraclitus, took the opposite position, arguing that change was impossible and existence was timeless and uniform. Parmenides considered nonexistence to be absurd, and thus asserted that it was impossible for something to come into existence out of nothing or for something to pass out of existence into nothing. He, therefore, rejected even the possibility for change and claimed that reality was an undifferentiated and unchanging whole.

The poem "On Nature" is the sole surviving work of Parmenides, and it only survives in a fragmented form. "On Nature" lays out two views of reality. The first describes reality as a *whole*, much in the same way as systems theory. In this description, change is impossible because existence is timeless, uniform, and unchanging. The competing view argues for a world based on sensory appearances. In this latter view, Parmenides argued that sensory faculties provide false and deceitful information that evidences change. At the heart of these conflicting positions is the contrast between sensory faculties (change) and pure reason (nonchange) as the means for determining truth—a conflict that would continue to dominate Western philosophy for the next two thousand years.

Socrates (469–399 BCE): Analytical Process Based on Observing the Physical World

Socrates arrived on the heels of Heraclitus and Parmenides. When studying Socrates, it is essential to remind ourselves that most of what remains in the record about Socrates comes to us from his student Plato. Plato's dialogues are among the most comprehensive accounts of Socrates to survive from antiquity, although, according to Sarah Kofman's book *Socrates: Fictions of a Philosopher*, it is unclear the degree to which Socrates himself is "hidden behind his 'best disciple,' Plato." While little is known about the historical Socrates, we certainly know about his state execution, the reasons for his execution, and his student Plato's awareness of these details.

Socrates' answer to the question of change was to side with Heraclitus accepting change and otherwise relying on the human 5-senses. Towards this end, Socrates is best known for his method of analysis, known today as the Socratic Method. His methodology makes Socrates a man of process and, therefore, a hero of the Game. Socrates argued that solving a problem was a matter of breaking it down into a series of questions, the answers to which would gradually provide the answer. Socrates used his method to expose the double standards of the leaders of the Athenian state. These unwelcome critiques earned Socrates the nickname "Gadfly" (the fly that bites the horse) from his student Plato. Socrates was loyal to his process in a way similar to the Game's patron martyr, Giordano Bruno, who was also executed by the Inquisition in 1600 for his loyalty to process.

Plato (428–348 BCE): Truth Exists Outside of Experience As Ideal Forms (Change Is the Fault of Our Senses)

The Greeks were beset with a problem. Clearly change was everywhere, but political authority required absolutes upon which to base that authority. Looking at it from the perspective of human nature, Plato's two main goals were, first, to maintain or increase his social position and, second, to not get killed like his teacher Socrates. Plato's answer to the question of change was to side with Parmenides and create a system of universal truths through a structure he called his theory of Forms. For Plato, these Forms existed beyond the realm of human senses, beyond the reach of change. In order to make his system of Forms work, Plato had to devalue the capacities of the human senses as untrustworthy and evil. Plato's attack on change (flux) can be found in the dialogue "Cratylus":

I believe that the primeval givers of names were undoubtedly like too many of our modern philosophers, who, in their search after the nature of things, are always getting dizzy from constantly going round and round, and then they imagine that the world is going round and round and moving in all directions; and this appearance, which arises out of their own internal condition, they supposed to be a reality of nature; they think that there is nothing stable or permanent, but only flux and motion, and that the world is always full of every sort of motion and change.

Plato saw where the integrity of process had got Socrates. With the ghost of Heraclitus still championing change, the Athenian state was breathing down Plato's neck, as it knew that Plato's words would be quick to turn public opinion. Without the claim to some form of unchanging truth, both statesman and philosopher were made powerless. What is a philosopher to do when assaults on self-preservation are closing in from both sides? Plato responded by creating a mechanism to secure truth amid change for the sake of state power and philosophical authority.

Plato's theory of Forms provided objective blueprints of perfection. These perfect Forms allowed Plato to sidestep the messy issue of change by asserting that information obtained through our five senses was a debased form of information that could not be trusted. Plato accomplished this task by making a distinction between nonmaterial abstract ideas and the world knowable through the five senses. Since, in this conceptualization, sensory experience is just the bastard child of truth, all concern for change is eliminated. The study of nonmaterial abstract ideas, Plato argued, was the only source of true knowledge. In viewing universal truth as a metaphysical construct not based on physical evidence, Plato's view represents the polar opposite of the Game.

The fact remains that Plato witnessed Socrates' execution and fully understood the relationship between Socrates' ideas and the displeasure those ideas caused the Athenian power brokers. To suggest that this experience did not influence his representation of Socrates' positions is unreasonable. So what was Plato to do? Continue his teacher's good fight and face execution by the state, or give the state what it wanted—the cover to continue acting selfishly—while appearing loyal to the state?

Aristotle (384–322 BCE): Universal Nature Is Embodied In All Things and Can Be Determined Through Analysis

Aristotle combined the best of Parmenides and Heraclitus so that analyzing physical evidence could go hand in hand with universal truth. Rather than arguing, like Plato, that universal Forms existed distinctly from the human senses, Aristotle argued that each physical thing embodied that thing's universal nature. Now there was universal truth for the powerful and sensory-based inquiry for the thoughtful.

Thomas Aquinas (1225–1274 CE): Universal Truth Is Alive

Reliance on universal truth by both church and state remained a constant theme throughout Western philosophy and didn't begin to lose steam until the Age of Enlightenment. We can see that the notions of change versus universality were alive and well in the Middle Ages through the writings of influential writers like Thomas Aquinas, and we can observe the continued impact of universality on Church doctrine. Aquinas distinguished four kinds of law: eternal, natural, human, and divine. Eternal law was the decree of God that governed all creation. Writing in Summa Theologica, Aquinas described Eternal Law by stating,

> … no one can know the eternal law, as it is in itself, except the blessed who see God in His Essence. But every rational creature knows it in its reflection, greater or less. For every knowledge of truth is a kind of reflection and participation of the eternal law, which is the unchangeable truth.

Natural law was the human "participation" in the eternal law, as discovered by reason. Notice the relationship between universality and reason. For Aquinas, universality and reason went hand in hand, just as they had for Aristotle, to bridge the gap between a changing world and a desire for unchanging truth.

There can be no question that both the Athenian state and the Catholic Church a millennium later derived their power from the authoritative association with universal or unchanging truth. Effectively, whoever controls truth controls power. We can see what happens when people like Socrates attempt to upset the relationship between truth and power. Notice, for instance, the emphasis placed on the relationship between language and authority described at the beginning of the Gospel of John:

> In the beginning was the Word, and the Word was with God, and the Word was God. He was with God in the beginning. Through him all things were made; without him nothing was made that has been made. In him was life, and that life was the light of all mankind. (John 1:1)

Those who control language control political power or, in the case of religion, control all creation; and as will be discussed in chapter 10, propaganda is about taking power where power is not due.

John Locke (1632–1704 CE): Empiricism Undermines Proof of Universal Forms

During the Age of Enlightenment, the championing of intuitive reason as the sole means of determining unchanging universal truth (God) began to fall apart. This trajectory has generally continued to the present day. The Game points to John Locke as a representative of this shift, but, of course, as Lovejoy points out, nothing is ever that black and white.

Locke broke the hold of intuitive reason over epistemology by asserting that we are born without innate ideas and that knowledge is, instead, determined by experience derived from sense perception. Locke opens his *An Essay Concerning Human Understanding* by stating

> It is an established opinion amongst some men that there are in the understanding certain *innate principals*; some primary notions, characters as it were, stamped upon the mind of man; which the soul

receives in its very first being, and brings it into the world with it. It would be sufficient to convince unprejudiced readers of the falseness of this supposition, if I should only show how men, barely by the use of their natural faculties, may attain to all the knowledge they have without the help of any innate impressions, and arrive at certainty, without any such notions of principals.

This was a truly radical and revolutionary set of ideas. This was the beginning of the crack in Western philosophy that would eventually usher in postmodernism a quarter of a millennia later. For the first time, humanity was being put in charge of truth without the need to control or sidestep change.

In Book II of his *Essay,* Locke goes on to state,

Let us then suppose the mind to be, as we say, white paper, void of all characters, without any ideas: How comes it to be furnished? Whence comes it by that vast store which the busy and boundless fancy of man has painted on it with an almost endless variety? When has it all the materials of reason and knowledge? To this I answer, in one word, from EXPERIENCE. In that all our knowledge is founded; and from that it ultimately derives itself. Our observation employed either, about external sensible objects, or about the internal operations of our minds perceived and reflected on by ourselves, is that which supplies our understandings with all the materials of thinking.

Notice how Locke's position directly contradicts Plato's doctrine of recollection, the idea that we are born possessing all knowledge and all we have to do is discover it using reason. Whether Plato's doctrine should be taken literally or not is the subject of debate. The idea goes like this: the soul once lived in "reality" where it knew everything, but then it became trapped in the body and forgot everything. The goal of recollection, Plato argued, is to get back to true knowledge. To do this, one must overcome the body. This doctrine implies the opposite of Locke's "white paper," as human senses are set aside in order to avoid the way change undermines authority.

Therefore, Locke's work represented a significant departure from Plato's notion that truth resided solely in universal Forms and that intuitive reason was the only vehicle for arriving at such truths. Locke, without knowing it, opened the gate to what would become known as the modern era.

The sophistication of modernism went beyond merely understanding knowledge as the product of observing the physical world; modern thinkers developed the notion that concepts were rarely made of single elements but were, in fact, the product of multiple elements in a state of interaction.

Rule # 37
What we know is learned from birth.

Friedrich Nietzsche (1844–1900 CE): No More Need for Universal Truth

The first modern thinker of importance to the Game is Friedrich Nietzsche, who called for the end of universal truth born of intuitive reasoning. Nietzsche's advance on universal truth should come as no surprise, considering that he was a big fan of Heraclitus and big detractor of Parmenides. As Nietzsche states in his work *Twilight of the Idols*,

> With the highest respect, I accept the name of *Heraclitus*. When the rest of the philosophic folk rejected the testimony of the senses because they showed multiplicity and change, he rejected their testimony because they showed things as if they had permanence and unity. Heraclitus too did the senses an injustice. They lie neither in the way the Eleatics believed, nor as he believed—they do not lie at all. What we *make* of their testimony, that alone introduces lies…But Heraclitus will remain eternally right with his assertion that being is an empty fiction. The "apparent" world is the only one: the "true" world is merely added by a lie.

What is so fascinating about the above quote is the way Nietzsche rejects the ideal of permanence while pivoting toward a critique of language itself: "They lie neither in the way the Eleatics believed, nor as he believed—they do not lie at all. What we *make* of their testimony, that alone introduces lies." Fifteen years earlier, Nietzsche wrote the essay "On Truth and Lie in an Extra-Moral

Sense," in which he critiques the illusion that sensory-based language has the capacity for determining truth. In this essay, Nietzsche states, "What is a word? It is the copy in sound of a nerve stimulus. But the further inference from the nerve stimulus to a cause outside of us is already the result of a false and unjustified application of the principal of sufficient reason." (81)

Nietzsche goes on to call into question the inherent relationship between words and meaning: "The various languages placed side by side show that with words it is never a question of truth, never a question of adequate expression; otherwise there would not be so many languages." (82) From here, Nietzsche begins to pick apart language itself:

> The "thing in itself" (which is precisely what the pure truth would be) is likewise something quite incomprehensible to the creator of language and something not in the least worth striving for. The creator only designates the relations of things to men, and for expressing these relations he lays hold of the boldest metaphors. To begin with, the nerve stimulus is transferred into an image: first metaphor. The image, in turn, is imitated in a sound: second metaphor. And each time there is a complete overlapping of one sphere, right into the middle of an entirely new and different one...we believe that we know something about the things themselves when we speak of trees, colors, snow and flowers; and yet we possess nothing but metaphors for things—metaphors which correspond in no way to the original entities. (82)

Based on this critique of language, Nietzsche turns to the nature of truth:

> What then is truth? A moveable host of metaphors, metonymies and anthropomorphisms: in short, a sum of human relations which have been poetically and rhetorically intensified, transferred and embellished, and which, after long usage, seem to people to be fixed, canonical and binding. Truths are illusions which we have forgotten are illusions; they are metaphors that have become worn out and have been drained of sensuous force, coins that have lost their embossing and are now considered as metal and no longer as coins. (84)

Complicating matters for Nietzsche are the advances being made in the scientific understanding of how the brain functions. Is the brain passively responding to stimulus, or is there some degree of cerebral anticipation? If so, what is the effect on perception of the human brain anticipating sensory stimulus? Furthermore, what exactly is the outcome when anticipation and illusion are combined to create reality?

The answer for Nietzsche was that language and the corresponding reality were nothing but a process. When we forget and begin believing the process is a thing, Nietzsche concluded, we are dreaming.

Rule # 38
Truth is an illusion we have forgot is an illusion.

Ferdinand de Saussure (1857–1913 CE): Language Is a System of Interacting Parts

It is all but impossible to find a language theorist today who has not built off of Saussure's ideas. Saussure formally proposed two essential ideas: a word, or *sign*, is a system of interacting parts, and the relationship between those parts is arbitrary.

Saussure was a systems theorist. In his *Course In General Linguistics*, Saussure states that "Language is a system of which all the parts can and must be considered as synchronistically interdependent." (86) In other words, meaning comes from context.

Since the Greeks, the question had been raised as to whether there was meaning between words and the things words describe. This was the subject of Plato's "Cratylus" dialogue and of interest to Nietzsche, as seen in the earlier section. If the relationship between words and things represented some *natural* causal relationship, then, as Nietzsche asked, why were so many languages needed to chase after essentially the same truth? What Saussure did was to peel back an additional layer of the analytical onion and investigate the word itself, which he labeled the *sign*. Saussure describes his notion of the linguistic sign by stating:

> The linguistic sign is not a link between a thing and a name, but between a concept and a sound pattern. The sound pattern is not an actual sound, for a sound is something physical. A sound pattern is the hearer's psychological impression of a sound, as given to him by the evidence of his senses...The sound pattern may thus be distinguished from the other element associated with it in a linguistic sign: the concept. (66)

So Saussure's *sign* is a system of two interacting parts: concept and sound pattern.

In keeping with systems theory and the demand that all elements of a system be accounted for, Saussure's work is more than merely academic. One of his translators, Roy Harris, explains that because of Saussure,

> Language is no longer regarded as peripheral to our grasp of the world we live in, but as central to it. Words are not mere vocal labels or communicational adjuncts superimposed upon an already given order of things. They are collective products of social interaction, essential instruments through which human beings constitute and articulate their world. This typically twentieth-century view of language has profoundly influenced developments throughout the whole range of human sciences. It is particularly marked in linguistics, philosophy, psychology, sociology and anthropology.

Notice what happens when the arbitrary nature of the linguistic sign is inserted into notions of political authority. If language is a social construct that is created and agreed upon by social convention, then value can be set collectively, rather than centrally as posited by Plato and others. From this perspective, universal truth is just an effort of those who seek centralized power to establish value or authority by sidestepping the need for collective agreement.

In his *Course in General Linguistics*, Saussure digs into the nature of language by analyzing the nature of the interaction of parts:

> In the language itself, there are only differences. Even more important than that is the fact that, although in general difference presupposes

positive terms between which the difference holds, in a language there are only differences, and no positive terms. Whether we take the signification or the signal, the language includes neither ideas nor sounds existing prior to the linguistic system, but only conceptual and phonetic differences arising out of that system. In a sign, what matters more than any idea or sound associated with it is what other signs surround it… A linguistic system is a series of phonetic differences matched with a series of conceptual differences. But the matching of a certain number of auditory signals and a similar number of items carved out from the mass of thought gives rise to a system of values. (118)

Saussure shows that a sign is not necessarily something that connects a word or name to a thing, but it is, in fact, something that connects a sound or image to a concept. The sound or image is called a *signifier*. The concept is called a *signified*. Meaning is produced not only by the relationship between the signifier and the signified, but also, crucially, by the position of the signifiers in relation to other signifiers in a given context.

When Saussure's theory is put together with Freud's (below), it is not difficult to see that the movement of signifiers, which generates meaning, must remain fundamentally unconscious. Meaning may only have a place in what Jacques Lacan calls "the signifying chain." From his seminar on Edgar Allan Poe's short story, The Purloined Letter, Lacan observes

This is what happens in repetition automatism… the subject follows the channels of the symbolic. But what is illustrated here is more gripping still: It is not only the subject, but the subjects, caught in their intersubjectivity, who line up—in other words, they are our ostriches, to whom we thus return here, and who, more docile than sheep, model their very being on the moment of the signifying chain that runs through them.

The signifier has primacy over the signified, which means that meaning is generated not by the normal meaning of a word but by the place the word has in a signifying chain.

Rule # 39
A word, or *sign*, is a system of interacting parts, and the relationship between those parts is arbitrary.

Sigmund Freud (1856–1939 CE): The Human Psyche Is a Set of Multiple Parts

Just as Saussure was giving birth to modern linguistics, Sigmund Freud was also changing the world by giving birth to modern psychoanalysis. And as with Saussure's work, language theorists continue today to draw on Freud's ideas for inspiration.

Like all modern thinkers, Freud changed the way we think about the human mind by understanding it not as a single thing but as a system of interacting parts. Freud's model contains three parts, which are

- **Id** (irrational hedonism): a selfish, primitive, childish, pleasure-oriented part of the personality with no ability to delay gratification;
- **Superego** (impractical moralism): internalized societal and parental standards of "good" and "bad," "right" and "wrong" behavior; and
- **Ego** (rational): the moderator between the id and the superego, which seeks compromises to pacify both and can be viewed as our "sense of time and place."

One of the biggest ideas to come from Freud's theories was that the complexity of the human mind includes irrational impulses. Freud was not only important in the fields of psychoanalysis and literary theory, but he was also read by nonacademics. While academia looked to Freud for ways to understand and improve the human condition, nonacademics, like the father of public relations, Edward Bernays, used Freud's ideas to justify their manipulations of the human condition (chapter 10). Bernays' work was later applied by Joseph Goebbels who was the Reich Minister of Propaganda in Nazi Germany from 1933 to 1945. The professed logic of these manipulators generally goes like this:

1. Freud explains how the human condition is marked by irrational impulses, both as individuals and in groups.
2. Irrational impulses undermine social order, specifically democracy.
3. Therefore, in the name of what is best for democracy, the masses need to be controlled by an unseen centralized force.

Can the irrational be tamed through education rather than through governmental/bureaucratic subterfuge? This depends on whom you ask. For manipulators like Bernays and Goebbels, the answer would be "no, there is nothing to do but manipulate." But, from the perspective of psychoanalysis, the opposite answer would be given: the human mind can learn to better understand itself and, in turn, to manage the irrational id through self-control. As with other examples of systems theory, looking at a situation from a systems perspective always opens up possibility for positive change.

Rule # 40
The human psyche is the product of interacting parts.

Karl Popper (1902–1994 CE): Process Is Everything

Popper was responsible for directing the conversation about truth back to the importance of process. His model of critical rationalism is the underlying model of the Game. Critical rationalism holds not only that claims to knowledge should be scrutinized but also that claimed knowledge must have the capacity to be demonstrated as false. Knowledge that is falsifiable is empirical; if it is not falsifiable, then it is nonempirical. This is the primary basis of how the Game determines what is and what is not metaphysics.

To this model, Popper added an awareness of how human nature influences the process. He contended that if the outcome of an experiment contradicts the theory, one should refrain from the temptation to avoid the contradiction. When an experiment provides an unexpected outcome, Popper argued, the natural response is to ignore the outcome by making it less falsifiable, which effectively creates a weak link within a larger theory. Requiring all ideas supporting a theory be falsifiable was Popper's way of eliminating such weak links.

Popper is of additional importance to the Game because of his views on the limitations of science, which mirror the conclusions of many postmodern language theorists. In effect, language has limited capacities, and, consequently, it cannot be used to attain universal truth. Writing in *Conjectures and Refutations: The Growth of Scientific Knowledge*, Popper states,

> The more we learn about the world, and the deeper our learning, the more conscious, specific, and articulate will be our knowledge of what we do not know, our knowledge of our ignorance. For this, indeed, is the main source of our ignorance—the fact that our knowledge can be only finite, while our ignorance must necessarily be infinite.

Popper was a great man who appreciated the power of humility when seeking truth.

Rule # 41
Knowledge is a finite representation of the infinite experience.

Jacques Derrida (1930–2004 CE): Context Is Everything

The Game's narrative of language theory ends with Jacques Derrida, not because he and other members of the Yale School taught at my university (UC, Irvine) but because his approach best honors the primary demand of systems theory: that the system set be all-inclusive, seek out all possible context, and, above all, strive toward integrity of process. Derrida's exhaustive search for context is precisely what systems theory demands when it requires a thorough study of the interaction of parts within each system—integrity of process through good-faith exhaustion of effort. Derrida's detractors are quick to identify his occasional lack of depth with respect to certain fields of inquiry. However, that is beside the point, as no one can be an expert in everything. The reason we study Derrida is not to worship his conclusions but to learn from the process he brought to the table.

The basic principle of Derrida's process of deconstruction is that societies rely on preconceived sets of meanings that are seen as absolute truths. It is on such preconceptions that societies base their relationship to language and meaning. Derrida argued that deconstruction denies the possibility of stable meaning or universal truth. Through the study of semiotics, Derrida began to deconstruct language, eloquently stating that words only have meaning because of their contrasting context with other words. Water is only hot because it is not cold, not because some universal truth dictated that water is hot independently from cold.

The model presented here is essentially a 2-dimentional linear line so that hot is on one end and cold is on the other. This study is designed for ages 16 and up and so this 2-dimentional model is appropriate. A more complex model for advance students is a 3-dimensional sphere where hot is one pole and cold is the opposite pole. Hot and cold are still intertwined but the possibilities for the relationship between poles and an infinitely variant context is unlimited.

Quantum mechanics visually represents a two-level quantum mechanical system as a "qubit." An example of a two-level quantum mechanical system is the *spin-up* and *spin-down* states of an electron, states that are oppositional but otherwise exist simultaneously.

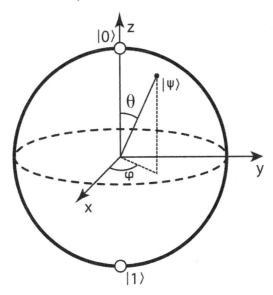

The above Bloch sphere is the product of Felix Bloch (1905 – 1983), a physicist and Nobel Prize winner. The application of the Bloch sphere accommodates the relationship between poles while also accommodating for the influences of outside context. When applied to language, a 3-dimentional spherical ("mixed Bloch") metaphor welcomes the influence of context so that context is as important as the extremes of either pole.

Donald D. Hoffman, professor of Cognitive Science, at my alma mater, UC, Irvine, is a leader in the new field of quantum linguistics. Visit his page (http://www.cogsci.uci.edu/~ddhoff/) for his books and downloadable papers on this exciting topic. Another excellent resource is the compendium of essays, Quantum Physics and Linguistics (Heunen). This book brings together physicist and linguists to discuss the way information flows among subsystems and the way this flow contributes to the make-up of the larger system. What I find so exciting is the way a 3-dimensional model of interconnectivity provides the potential for the very kind of nuance demanded by Derrida's process.

What Derrida represents to the Game is an exhaustive view of language that makes a good-faith effort to study relationships. In his essay "Infrastructures and Systematicity," Rodolphe Gasché describes Derrida's process as follows:

> But deconstruction which for many has come to designate the content and style of Derrida's thinking, reveals to even a superficial examination, a well-ordered procedure, a step-by-step type of argumentation based on an acute awareness of level-distinctions, a marked thoroughness and regularity…Deconstruction must be understood, we contend, as the attempt to "account," in a certain manner, for a heterogeneous variety or manifold of nonlogical contradictions and discursive equalities of all sorts that continues to haunt and fissure even the *successful* development of philosophical arguments and their systematic exposition.

For the Game, Derrida represents integrity and exhaustion of process.

Building on Saussure's notion of difference ("In language there are only differences"), Derrida argues the following in his essay "Différance":

> Force itself is never present; it is only a play of difference and quantities. There would be no more force in general without the difference between forces…Which, according to the same logic, according to logic itself, does not exclude that philosophy lives *in* and *on difference*,

thereby binding itself to the *same*, which is not the identical...Thus one could reconsider all the pairs of opposites on which philosophy is constructed and on which our discourse lives, not in order to see opposition erase itself but to see what indicates that each of the terms must appear as the *différance* of the other.

Some have argued that Derrida was a philosophical nihilist who was attempting to destroy meaning, when, in fact, the opposite is clearly evident in his writings. "No stone left unturned" is a far better characterization of Derrida's efforts. What makes Derrida's approach exhaustive is his insistence that meaning and context cannot be separated. The study of context is the study of the interaction between the parts of a system; this makes Derrida a hero of the Game.

Although I have heaped all this praise onto Derrida, teachers should not hand out copies of a Derrida essay to sixteen-year-olds with instructions to read it for the next class. Such a tactic is most likely to permanently scare students for life. Instead, keep it simple by asking, "Can the idea of hot exist in the absence of the corresponding concept cold?" With this simple question, you will turn on the brains of your students. Wrapping their minds around this simple question provides ample challenge for the average tenth grader and leaves open the opportunity to further explore the world of hidden meaning.

Rule # 42
Language is a complex system built around the forces of difference.

Systems theory provides a set of tools to help make sense of all the interacting parts that collectively come together and create language. Marko Juvan says it best in his paper "On Literariness: From Post-structuralism to Systems Theory":

> Systems theory in and for the study of literature, such as proposed in Schmidt's *Empirische Literaturwissenschaft* (*Empirical Study of Literature*), neither reduces literariness to a textual property nor it denies the fact, that a text as a material "scheme" and basis for

processing has something to do with its own (and other text's) cultural and social effects. Instead, systems theory has elaborated a series of interdisciplinary conceptual tools, which are able to describe the subtlest socio-historical, psychic, linguo-pragmatic and actionable (behavioral) ramifications, in which literariness can be intended, planned, textualized, and grasped, i.e., contexts of the construction and functioning of literariness.

Language is not simple. Not only do we operators of language bring a big influence to bear, but the operation of language itself also provides significant influence. Being aware of these influences provides high-school students with a lifetime of respect for the complex contextual understanding such awareness offers.

Chapter Bibliography

Aquinas, Thomas. 2006. *Summa Theologica*, Part I-II. Translated by Fathers of the English Dominican Province, 1920. The Project Gutenberg eBook # 17897: http://www.gutenberg.org/ebooks/17897

Bernays, Edward. (1928) 2004. *Propaganda*. New York: Ig. 37

Derrida, Jacques. 1968. "Différence" *Critical Theory Since 1965*. Ed Hazard Adams & Leroy Searle. Tallahassee, Florida, University Presses of Florida. 129-30. http://hydra.humanities.uci.edu/derrida/diff.html

de Saussure, Ferdinand. (1916) 1977. *Course in General Linguistics*. Edited by C. Bally and A. Sechehaye. Translated by Roy Harris. La Salle, Il, Open Court.

Freud, Sigmund. 1920. *A General Introduction to Psychoanalysis*. Translated by G. Stanley Hall. New York: Boni and Liveright.

———. (1930) 1989. *Civilization and Its Discontents*. Translated by James Strachey. London: W. W. Norton.

Gasché, Rodolphe. "Infrastructures and Systematicity," in John Sallis (ed.), Deconstruction and Philosophy (Chicago & London: University of Chicago Press, 1987), pp. 3–4

Harris, Roy. 1988. *Language, Saussure, and Wittgenstein: How to Play Games with Words*. Routledge. 86

Heunen, Chris ed., *Quantum Physics and Linguistics: A Compositional, Diagrammatic Discourse*. Oxford University Press. April 22, 2013

Juvan, Marko. 2000. "On Literariness: From Post-Structuralism to Systems Theory." 10. *CLCWeb: Comparative Literature and Culture* 2 (2). http://docs.lib.purdue.edu/clcweb/vol2/iss2/1/

Kofman, Sarah. 1998. *Socrates: Fictions of a Philosopher*. Translated by Catherine Porter. Ithaca, NY: Cornell University Press. 34

Lacan, Jacques. 1996. *Écris*. New York, W.W. Norton & Company. Trans Bruce Fink. 21 https://archive.org/details/Lacan-Ecrits

Locke, John. (1690) 2004. *An Essay Concerning Humane Understanding, Volume I. MDCXC, Based on the 2nd Edition, Books I. and II.* The Project Gutenberg EBook # 10615: http://www.gutenberg.org/ebooks/10615

Lovejoy, Arthur O. 1936. *The Great Chain of Being*. Cambridge, MA: Harvard University Press. 3-4

Nietzsche, Friedrich. (1873) 1979. "On Truth and Lie in the Extra-Moral Sense." *Phylosophy and Truth: Selections from Nietzsche's Notebooks of the early 1870's*. Translated by Daniel Breazeale. Humanitis Press International.

———. (1888) 1990. *Twilight of the Idols and the Anti-Christ: or How to Philosophize with a Hammer*. Lexido and The Project Gutenberg: http://www.lexido.com/EBOOK_TEXTS/TWILIGHT_OF_THE_IDOLS_.aspx?S=4

Plato. 2008. *Cratylus*. Translated by Benjamin Jowett. The Project Gutenberg EBook #1616: http://www.gutenberg.org/ebooks/1616

Popper, Karl. 1962. *CONJECTURES AND REFUTATIONS: The Growth of Scientific Knowledge*. New York, Basic Books. 28. http://xxsy.library.nenu.edu. cn/pluginfile.php/1066/mod_resource/content/1/%5BKarl_Popper%5D_ Conjectures_and_Refutations_The_Gro(Bookos.org)%20(1).pdf

CHAPTER 9

Logic

> All men are mortal. Socrates was mortal.
> Therefore, all men are Socrates.
> WOODY ALLEN, *LOVE AND DEATH*

Logic is the algebra of language. As old as the hills, it goes back at least as far as the Ancient Greeks and specifically Aristotle's set of texts called the *Organon*. Today, there are a number of different types of logic, including the following:

- Formal
- Informal
- Symbolic
- Mathematical

Our study will focus on informal logic, the argument form, and logical fallacies.

Argument Form

An argument's form is essentially an if/then statement that looks something like this (Δ = Therefore):

A. All humans are mortal.

B. Socrates is human.

C. Δ, Socrates is mortal.

If A and B are true, then C must also be true. Steps one and two are examples of *logical statements*, and step three is the resulting *conclusion*.

Pulling together all the parts of an argument and organizing them into a formal order is an excellent way to ensure that your argument is

- **Consistent**: no part of an argument contradicts another part;
- **Valid**: the conclusion is supported by the premises; and
- **Complete**: if a theorem is true, it can be proven.

The Rules of logic serve the integrity of process by ensuring that all values, beliefs, and principles are driven by sound thinking. Logical fallacies specifically identify the ways the mind can be emotionally manipulated and then *prohibits* such manipulation. For example, it is emotionally easy to believe something is true simply because everyone else believes it is true. However, not only is getting caught up in the enthusiasm of a crowd no basis for belief, it also presents situations that are ripe for outside manipulation. A government, for instance, may use the notion of patriotism to sell war to an otherwise-disinterested nation. In this way, logic can be viewed as the product of analyzing human psychology for the purpose of preventing manipulation.

Logic takes on a more prominent role in the Game not just as the rules of sound thinking but also as the toolbox of propagandists. With every prohibitive rule of logic, there is a corresponding proactive tool of propaganda. For instance, the above example is known as the fallacy of the populous. While this logical rule prohibits arguments from using widespread belief as proof of something being true, it is exactly what advertising executives or public-relations specialists use to sway opinion.

For most of recorded time, Europeans thought the Earth to be flat. Then, everyone but the Flat Earth Society advanced to believing that the Earth was round and at the center of our solar system. (For the sake of full disclosure, I am a member of the Flat Earth Society, London chapter.) For long periods of time, the Catholic Church was willing to torture and kill people to maintain this popular belief. After Copernicus but before Galileo, Giordano Bruno, a Catholic monk and patron martyr of the Game, looked at the night sky through a crude telescope and determined that the Earth was, in fact, a satellite of the sun—in direct contradiction to the Church's conception. He further argued that since God was infinite and creation was made in His image, then creation, too, must be infinite; therefore, there must be life on other planets just as here on Earth.

Bruno's beliefs would not have been so inflammatory if the emergent "Protestant problem" had not existed. The Catholic Church's absolute hold on power was under threat, and it was willing to do whatever was necessary to maintain power. Since questions of cosmology were part of that political struggle, Bruno walked into a political firestorm. Despite the controversy at the time surrounding cosmology, Bruno spoke his mind because he believed that he was right and that his friend Pope Pius V would bail him out if things went too far.

Bruno was right about many things. But, being human, he was also wrong about a few things, one of which being the Pope's willingness to protect him from the Inquisition amid the Catholics' battle with the Protestants. Bruno was burned alive at the stake on February 17, 1600. Logic is a powerful tool, but so is human nature, especially when corrupted by the influence of centralized power.

Rule # 43
All statements must adhere to the rules of logic.

Logical Fallacies

A logical fallacy is an effort to divert attention away from evidence and analysis by preying on the emotional weaknesses of human nature. In the parlance of academic logic, fallacies are incorrect forms of reasoning in argumentation that result in misconception. Fallacies exploit emotional triggers in the audience, often by taking advantage of social relationships between people (peer pressure).

The difference between the way logical fallacies are taught in school and the following approach is that logic is usually taught from the perspective of good-faith error. In other words, relying on a fallacy during an argument is a form of mistake. Here, the opposite approach is taken, namely, that the use of fallacies is part of an intentional effort by the advertising, public-relations, and communications industries to manipulate the relationship between language and the physical world on behalf of paying clients.

Appeals to Authority: Just as Lord Acton observed a corrupting relationship between power and human nature, people often believe in the opinions of a speaker simply because that individual is endowed by society with some form of authority, regardless of any actual qualification. In this way, a speaker's authority itself becomes a tool of propaganda.

There are all kinds of ways in which the illusion of authority can be created where none exists. One example comes from the Museum of Creation and Earth History in Santee California. When you enter the museum, you are greeted by an individual wearing a white lab coat. This garment of science gives the wearer an air of scientific authority. After all, everyone knows that people who wear lab coats are highly educated scientists. How do we know this? Because our family doctor wears a white lab coat and the actors playing scientists on TV also wear white lab coats. Of course, a white lab coat does not a scientist make, but those who are blind to this are open to manipulation, which is entirely the point.

Rule # 44
Logic prohibits appeals to authority whereby arguments are based on the testimony of an unqualified person.

Appeals to the People: Just as people can be swayed by manufactured authority, so, too, can we be swayed by arguments based on common beliefs or traditional practices, that is, popular belief. Because this fallacy preys on a weakness of human nature—the desire to be part of a group—it is a powerful tool of propaganda.

Students can be drawn into this discussion by asking them for examples of fallacies based on appeals to the people found in everyday advertising. Some examples include the following:

- The Ford F-150 is the best-selling truck in America; therefore, it is the best truck.
- More people prefer the taste of Pepsi to Coca-Cola; therefore, Pepsi is better than Coke.

If your students watch TV, they will be at the ready with additional examples.

Rule # 45
Logic prohibits appeals to the people whereby arguments are based on common beliefs or traditional practices.

Appeals to Consequences: This fallacy is yet another example of diverting an audience's attention away from evidence and analysis. Rather than looking at the evidence, the audience is directed to the positive or negative consequences of accepting an idea. These positive or negative consequences themselves may be contrived and may be part of the manipulation. With the mind made busy worrying about consequences, it is diverted from analyzing evidence.

One of the greatest canards used by the US Chamber of Commerce is concern over lost US jobs. The fact is that this prestigious body has one of the longest track records of furthering the export of US jobs to developing nations for the explicit purpose of lowering labor costs so as to raise member profits. In addition, during the Reagan administration, corporate law was changed on behalf of hedge funds so that employee pensions were shifted from being a liability owed to future pensioners to a balance-sheet asset. With pension funds moved into the asset column, corporate raiders like Mitt Romney were able to buy a company with inexpensive junk bonds and then liquidate the pension funds for profit while loading up the company's balance sheet with junk debt— all the while moving US jobs offshore to low-wage nations. The consequence of this theft was to ruin the retirement hopes of employees along with a large swath of the overall US economy.

Ask students for an example of a possible consequence that they think is more important than the evidence. Is this consequence a guaranteed result, or is it merely speculative? What is the relationship between consequence and evidence or analysis?

Rule # 46
Logic prohibits appeals to consequences whereby arguments are based on the positive or negative consequences of acceptance.

Appeals to Emotion: This is an easy fallacy to teach because it has so many flavors:

- Appeal to emotion
- Appeal to pity
- Appeal to novelty
- Appeal to prejudice
- Appeal to patriotism
- Appeal to aesthetics
- Appeal to hope

The above list provides students with a pattern, which not only helps to demonstrate variations of emotion but also sets up the opportunity to add/drop items in the list.

Human nature predisposes us to being driven by certain emotions. Since the average person spends little time on self-reflection, there is little awareness as to the influence of emotions. Patriotism, for example, is an emotion that is often embraced without any idea of how it functions within the human psyche or how it can be used to control an individual's thinking.

In 2015, it was revealed that the Pentagon paid the National Football League and other sports leagues to "honor US soldiers" at games. According the New York Times,

> Over the past four years, the Army National Guard and other branches have signed agreements worth $6.8 million with teams from the National Football League, Major League Baseball and other sports leagues that included "paid-for patriotism," said Senators Jeff Flake and John McCain, Republicans of Arizona.
>
> It is unclear exactly how much of that marketing money paid for ceremonies with names like "Salute to Service" and other recognition of

the armed forces. And the report conceded that $6.8 million was just a sliver of the $53 million the military spent on advertising with sports teams during that time. (Huetteman)

These payments to sporting leagues represent a transparent attempt to sway public opinion about US foreign policy by appealing to emotion rather than to evidence-based analysis. This form of propaganda also conflates the subject of US foreign policy with the individuals sent to fight—another effort to distract thought away from analysis.

Have students collectively make an exhaustive list of all the emotions that can be used to distract people from analysis. After a list has been created, students can form groups, choose one emotion, and provide examples of how that emotion might be used to distract an individual from thinking. These examples can be creative or taken from news reports.

Rule # 47
Logic prohibits appeals to emotion whereby arguments are based on emotional manipulation.

Appeals to Ignorance (*Argumentum ad Ignorantiam*): This particular logical fallacy prohibits arguments based on a lack of evidence. Just because there is no evidence that an idea is true does not necessarily mean the idea is false This fallacy should give heart to those interested in UFOs, as a lack of evidence is the bread and butter of UFO deniers, who argue that since there is no agreed upon evidence, then UFOs do not exist.

Rule # 48
Logic prohibits appeals to ignorance whereby a lack of evidence implies the opposite is true or false.

Appeals Against the Person: Like the previous fallacy, appeals against the person come in a range of flavors and are otherwise known as "*ad hominem* attacks." This kind of fallacy runs parallel to the fallacy of false correlation. The basic form of the fallacy deals with attacking the person as a way of distracting the audience from analyzing evidence. The nature of such attacks includes the following:

- Appeal against the person;
- Appeal against the person, abusive;
- Appeal against the person, circumstantial;
- Appeal against the person, guilt by association; and
- Appeal against the person, *tu quoque* (you, too).

An abusive *ad hominem* attack goes after the person's character so that the individual's character becomes the focus of the debate rather than the underlying evidence. A circumstantial *ad hominem* attack focuses on the motivations of the person. A guilt-by-association *ad hominem* attack redirects inquiry toward the associations of a person rather than the evidence. A *tu quoque* attack transfers the weakness of the attacker onto the attacked. Using appeals against the person is a simple matter of analyzing your own weaknesses and then planning the best way to preempt the exposure of these weaknesses by the opposition.

Rule # 49
Logic prohibits appeals against the person whereby arguments are based on attacking the person rather than his or her argument.

False Cause: This fallacy prohibits arguments based on correlation in the absence of causality, that is, conflating causality with correlation. It can be applied in various situations:

- **False cause by association:** A logical fallacy that prohibits arguments where *A* is connected to *B* because of a meaningless characteristic that is otherwise commonly understood.
- **False cause by place** (*Post hic, ergo propter hic*; after here, therefore because of here): A logical fallacy that prohibits arguments where *B* is similar to *A* simply because *B* shares a physical proximity to *A*.
- **False cause by time** (*Post hoc, ergo propter hoc*; after this, therefore because of this): A logical fallacy that prohibits arguments where *A* caused event *B* simply because *A* preceded *B* in time.

Rule # 50
Logic prohibits false-cause arguments that conflate causality with correlations of association, place, and time.

Oversimplification: This fallacy is tied directly back to the last chapter's discussion of systems theory and is similar to the fallacy of either/or. Here, the fallacy is based on proposing a solution without taking into account all relevant factors. Oversimplification is the act of limiting or outright eliminating evidence.

For example, any argument that identifies race as the cause of anything is, by definition, an oversimplification because race is nothing more than a contrived form of human difference; that is, the differences of race only exist in the mind. By making an oversimplification based on race, the conversation avoids discussions of culture. By avoiding discussions of culture, the conversation avoids ideas of cause and effect, which in turn avoids notions of privilege and questions of how and why dominant cultures oppress weaker ones.

Rule # 51
Logic prohibits oversimplification whereby arguments are based on proposing a solution without taking into account all relevant factors.

Slippery Slope: Slippery-slope arguments claim the idea being discussed will begin a chain of events that will inevitably lead to some undesirable result. This fun fallacy is known to every minority. For instance, the Reverend Lou Sheldon of the Traditional Values Coalition tells us that allowing two people of the same sex to marry leads to bestiality. Broadening the definition of marriage to include same-sex couples opens the door to any contrived scenario an opponent to gay marriage wishes to deploy. The fallacy of the slippery slope is an effective tool of anyone who wishes to obstruct change.

Have students make a list of cultural changes that have taken place in the United States. In groups, they can choose a particular cultural change and then use a slippery-slope argument to take a position against the change. When the presentations are completed, note for the class how, in each case, the slippery-slope argument drew attention away from the underlying evidence driving the change.

Rule # 52
Logic prohibits slippery-slope arguments where the idea being discussed will begin a chain of events that will inevitably lead to some undesirable result.

False Dilemma of Either/Or: An argument based on the existence of only two options is suspiciously false because life is rarely so neat and tidy. Such a position implies that the speaker is omnipotent and knows all possible options. This either/or position is one of the best "red flags" for quickly identifying the weakness of an argument. This is good, since it may be one of the most often used fallacies.

The fallacy of false dilemma goes hand in hand with appeals to ignorance. To be able to manipulate a person by way of a false dilemma, that person must be ignorant of the subject's complexity and unaware that a third way of analysis is possible.

The way the US war on terror is framed is a good example of the fallacy of either/or in practice. In 2001, President Bush often pushed the line "You're either with us or against us in the fight against terror." The implication here is that anyone not willing to follow the US lead on foreign policy must, by default, be a terrorist. What such an analysis leaves out is the possibility of a third option, such as a desire to treat violence as a matter of law enforcement driven by evidence-based process.

More importantly, without the constraints of either/or, there is more room to analyze the situation in more depth and to ask exactly why people are willing to kill themselves in support of a cause. To further diminish this more complex line of inquiry, Bush also added the notion that those seeking to do harm to the United States do so because they "hate our freedoms." By combining the fallacy of either/or with the characterization of opposing violence as ideological in the context of the jingoism, all thought about the causes of terrorism are effectively stripped away from public debate. Without a robust inquiry into the cause, the United States can conduct its foreign policy free of the constraints of evidence, which is good for the stockholders of General Dynamics, Northrop Grumann, Boeing and Lockheed Martin.

In 2002, I had my students on the Hoopa Indian Reservation in northern California read an antiwar speech given by US Senator Robert Byrd on the floor of the US Senate. The gist of Byrd's speech was his opposition to the impending attack on Iraq by US forces. The next day, the local sheriff, in uniform with his badge, gun, showed up in my classroom; with veins pulsating from his neck, he asked what the hell I was teaching his son in my classroom. Clearly, there is nothing wrong with reading a speech given from the floor of the US Senate, and when I showed the sheriff a copy of the speech and explained its context, he backed off; it was clear to me that his son had played him by not telling his father the full story. I fully understand why some teachers would want to avoid such confrontations.

In the world of sports, the practice of either/or happens when one team is pitted against another. Sport is a form of escapism. In his book *Civilization and its Discontents*, Sigmund Freud identified sport as one of the primary ways we compensate for living within the constraints of society. Why is the fallacy of either/or so effective and often applied even in situations where there is no obvious need for propaganda? Because it feels good to have a complete understanding of complex issues, even if that understanding is contrived—just like a mind-altering drug.

Rule # 53
Logic prohibits false dilemmas of either/or whereby arguments are based on there being only two possible options, of which only one is correct.

Equivocation: The act of *equivocation* is about taking advantage of ambiguity in the mind of the audience. In the context of a logical fallacy, equivocation is so closely tied to one of my favorite tools of propaganda, *conflation*, that I have a hard time keeping them separate. To fallaciously equivocate is to apply two different meanings to the same word so as to obscure the distinction between those meanings. To fallaciously conflate is to mix up several distinct issues, often (but not always) with the aim of changing or redirecting away from the topic. So, it is reasonable to say that conflation can be a form of equivocation.

The bottom line is that propagandists who practice equivocation are essentially hustlers, like those who work a shell game out on the street where three shells and a dried pea are used to prey on audience confusions.

This idea can be demonstrated to students by identifying a word with two meanings that is used twice in the same context. Follow with a definition that would be appropriate for one use of the word but not for the other. Another way of doing the same exercise is to translate the sentence that twice uses the word from English into another language. The dual meanings of the same word will be exposed during translation. Start with an example most students will identify with, such as the following:

> I have the *right* to watch *Family Guy*. Therefore it's *right* for me to watch the show. So, I think I'll binge watch *Family Guy* on Netflix tonight instead of studying for tomorrow's exam.

In the above case, the word "right" has two distinct meanings: first, as a moral principal and, second, as the notion of appropriateness. By equivocating these two different meanings, the speaker is granting the decision to blow off studying an air of moral principal and thereby escaping the responsibility of reasonable time management.

Rule # 54
Logic prohibits equivocations whereby arguments are based on applying two different meanings to the same word.

Hasty Generalizations: An argument commits the fallacy of generalization when it attempts to assert a minority characteristic on the majority of a group. The antidote for this form of confusion is to ensure that the initial sampling of the group is large enough to sustain a generalized characteristic. From the propagandist's point of view, the improper sampling of a group is an intentional act of manipulation and a proactive part of the propagandist's toolbox.

This frequently used tool of propaganda is regularly applied to a subgroup of an existing minority for the purpose of demonizing the entire group. Poor people buy their illegal drugs on the street, whereas well-to-do people have their drugs delivered to their office by well-dressed dealers. Statistics make it clear that far more cocaine is consumed by upper-class white people than by poorer African Americans. However, the evening news never shows a cocaine bust of lawyers or Wall Street executives, despite the fact that these groups are the larger consumers of this drug. Based on what they see, people draw the conclusion that our nation's drug problem is confined to poor inner-city minorities.

Rule # 55
Logic prohibits hasty generalizations whereby arguments assert that something is true for the whole by ignoring the exception.

False Compositions: This fallacy is an attempt to assert that what is true of a system's parts is true of the system's whole. As such, false composition is similar to hasty generalization. The common phrase "What is true of the parts may *not* be true of the whole" seeks to undermine false composition. Another way of saying the same thing is "The whole is more than the sum of its parts." This is systems theory in action.

Sport is always a good metaphor when working with students. The whole concept of a Dream Team operates under the assumption that combining exceptional players into a single team will produce exceptional results. The 2008 Dallas Cowboys is one example of this idea gone awry. This team combined Zach Thomas, Terrell Owens, and an emerging Miles Austin and added Felix Jones, along with Martellus Bennett, to complement Marion Barber and Jason Witten. Rather than dominating their opponents as expected, their season ended with a 9–7 record and a four-game losing streak. Not only can a false composition lead to a break down in logic, it can also cause havoc at the betting window.

Rule # 56
Logic prohibits false compositions whereby arguments assert that what is true of the parts is true of the whole.

False Divisions: This fallacy takes the reverse form of false composition. Whereas a false composition asserts that what is true of a system's parts is true of the whole, the fallacy of division asserts that what is true of the whole is also true of the parts. Just because humans are the only animal capable of philosophical thought, this does not mean that all humans are capable of such thought.

One of the many things I learned as an inner-city high-school English teacher is that every student demographic includes gifted students. Yes, the majority of poor students drop out freshman year, and those who remain score academically lower than their more wealthy counterparts. But amid this general climate of lower academic achievement are amazingly gifted kids. One of my Bell High School students went from his inner-city school of five thousand to University of California, Irvine, where he completed a double major in English and French in three years with a 4.0 GPA.

Rule # 57
Logic prohibits false divisions whereby arguments assert that what is true of the whole is true of the parts.

False Analogy: Like false division and false composition, false analogy also has a direct tie to systems theory. Logic prohibits false analogies whereby arguments assert that if two or more things are alike in some respects, then they are also alike in other respects (see causation versus correlation). To use the terminology of set theory, what is true of one part in a set is true of all parts of that set. Propagandists use this tool when denigrating a minority group by identifying a negative trait of an individual and applying it to the entire minority.

One example of a false analogy is the attempt to paint all gay men as pedophiles. Here, the use of false analogy is married to the fallacy of the slippery slope to create the archetype of the gay monster. One silver lining of the Catholic Church's scandal regarding sociopathic pedophilic clergy who engaged in aggravated sexual assault on children is that it makes the charge against gay people seem quaint. Being a sexual monster, it is now clear, is an equal-opportunity condition open to all orientations: gay, straight, and the celibate.

Rule # 58
Logic prohibits false analogies whereby arguments assert that if two or more things are alike in some respects, then they are also alike in other respects (see false cause).

Circular Reasoning: Circular reasoning arises when arguments use what they are trying to prove as part of the proof of that thing. This fallacy feels like home to me, as I was an evangelical Christian for the first twenty-one years of my life. Up until the point of my conversion, I was convinced that God was the one true God because the Bible said so; and I knew that the Bible was true because it said so. This created a nice tidy package of circular reasoning.

I must say that circular reasoning is emotionally seductive because it presents the believer with a sense of omnipotence, which is also why circular reasoning is so dangerous to human systems. For the believer, breaking the circular belief chain requires the application of the third Test of Discovery: can the evidence be negated by testing? This step requires evidence to hold the possibility of being proved false. Unfortunately, metaphysical believers are not going to let go of any link from their circular belief chain.

Ask students to look for an argument or a question in which the author uses an assumption as part of the conclusion.

Rule # 59
Logic prohibits circular reasoning whereby arguments use what they are trying to prove as part of the proof.

Straw Man: This fallacy involves the effort to derail an opponent's argument by overstating the augment so as to attack the overstatement and, thereby, discredit the argument. This fallacy is a common tool used to discredit an opponent's position through the act of "getting out in front" of an opponent's otherwise-valid point through misrepresentation. If your opponent is concerned that the Pentagon has never been audited and is otherwise shielded from audit through thousands of separate accounting systems, all you need to do is claim the opponent is against policies that support a strong national defense.

Ask students to identify a response that misrepresents an opponent's argument in order to defeat it more easily.

Rule # 60
Logic prohibits straw man reasoning whereby an argument misrepresents the opposing position.

Red Herring: Similar to a straw-man argument, a red herring is when someone attempts to sidetrack attention away from an issue by introducing a seemingly related but actually unrelated issue as a means of distraction. Use of red herrings is a common device in mystery stories. The red-herring metaphor is easy to remember because it comes from the smelly, and therefore distracting, nature of cooked herring.

The arguments put forth by the public-education-reform industry provide a good example of a red herring argument in action. To begin with, there is no education crisis in K–12 public education, except for the intentional shifting of revenues away from public education through changes in the tax code. When academic performance is viewed as a bell curve, the top 66 percent of students and schools is doing fine. It is in the bottom 33 percent that there is serious trouble. The reason this is not discussed is that it is all but impossible to ignore the role poverty plays in academic achievement when we just focus on the lower third of student performance. The problem with discussing poverty is that combating the effects of poverty is expensive; that is, it is more expensive to provide poor children the same education opportunity as wealthy children. Furthermore, we do not discuss the causes of poverty, specifically the lack of economic opportunity, because poverty is essential to our economic model, which relies on it to keep wages low and profits high.

According to a 2015 report by the Southern Education Foundation, "Low-income students are now a majority of the schoolchildren attending the nation's public schools, according to this research bulletin. The latest data collected from the states by the National Center for Education Statistics (NCES), show that 51 percent of the students across the nation's public schools were low income in 2013."

Poverty impacts academic performance is numerous ways. Public education is set up to be the perfect model of democracy with local school boards working with parents. This model is set up like a table with four legs: students, parents, teachers, and administrators. If any one of these legs is unsound, the entire model falters. Poorer people tend to lack the skills, the time, and the cultural history to take an active role in the politics of the local public-school system. The result is that the schools that serve predominantly poor communities lack the necessary checks and balances provided by articulate parents with enough disposable time to take an active role in school governance. The result is schools, and even entire school districts, that are effectively free of meaningful oversight. This lack of accountability leaves administrators free to serve their own political ambitions. Read my book, *Road to Belmont*, which chronicles my journey from classroom teacher to California state investigator for examples of how a lack of parental involvement has resulted in our nation's second-largest school district failing to reach its goals.

Claiming that US public education is in a state of "crisis" is an example of the logical fallacy of false composition because it applies characteristics of failure by a minority of underperforming students onto the majority of students. Meanwhile, the problem is primarily localized. However, by focusing on an entire system in crisis, the cause of poverty is ignored, and profit-driven "solutions" are accepted. This distraction away from poverty allows for-profit interests to capture large chunks of public education funding in the name of reform.

Have students look for arguments in which the speaker redirects the discussion away from the cause of a problem as a self-serving distraction.

Rule # 61
Logic prohibits red herrings whereby arguments sidetrack the opposition by introducing an unrelated issue that seems relevant as a means of distraction.

Inconsistency: Logic prohibits the fallacy of inconsistency whereby an argument is based on a set of ideas that simultaneously cannot be true. For instance, when President Ronald Reagan came into office in 1981, the United States was the largest lender in the world. By the time Reagan left office, the United States was the largest borrower in the world. Reagan campaigned on the promise of producing a balanced budget without sacrificing domestic spending while, at the same time, increasing defense spending without raising taxes. He kept part of his promises by spending tax dollars on the machines of war; he just ignored the other side of his pledge where he promised to do so without deficit spending.

Have students look for political statements that include assertions that cannot be simultaneously valid.

Rule # 62
Logic prohibits inconsistency whereby an argument is based on a set of ideas that cannot simultaneously be true.

False Compromises: The middle ground between two competing ideas is not necessarily the best outcome. This notion that the middle ground is inherently valuable is useful for those who wish to attack an opponent but who, otherwise, have no game. False compromise uses the validity of an opposing argument to give credence to the opposite position. The underlying idea is that opinions represent extremes and that truth is always the product of intellectual compromise.

Say you believe that the Earth is flat and you are debating this point with a "round earther." You have only your misunderstanding and paranoia as the basis of your position, so you claim that the truth lies somewhere between a flat earth and a round one: a concave or convex-shaped earth.

Rule # 63
Logic prohibits false compromises whereby arguments assert that the most valid conclusion is the best compromise between two competing positions.

Appeals to History: A great deal of medical practice before the Age of Enlightenment was based on past practice in the absence of testing. The justification for a practice was that it had always been done that way.

The religious or cultural traditions that judge people as socially unfit are interesting studies because the primary motivation is resistance to change amid shifting privilege. The result is an effort to defend the indefensible by drawing on the most absurd justifications.

African Americans have a long history of being marginalized as human beings so that they might be exploited without financial or social cost. Women have a long history of being marginalized away from positions of power. The Roma, homosexuals, and the disabled were all given a place next to the Jews by Nazi Germany. Notice the long road to acceptance these groups walked before they found protection by the state. In the case of the Rome, even in 2016 they are still being treated by the French as undesirables. In all these cases, there was no physical evidence driving society's effort to marginalize these groups, which leaves wide open the observation that socioeconomic marginalization is a direct product of maintaining privilege.

These social efforts to marginalize others were all driven by a majority willing to accept the persecution of others for personal gain or for the maintenance of privilege during times of shrinking opportunity. Men are happy to repress women if it means less competition for advancement and pay. Whites are happy to allow the repression of racial minorities for the same reasons that drive gender inequality: less competition for the spoils of society. All of this is done without the support of physical evidence; all the while, proponents claim repression is justified because of historical precedent.

Rule # 64
Logic prohibits appeals to history whereby arguments are based on the concept "We should do this now because it's always been done that way."

Appeals to Logic: This fallacy prohibits any argument that asserts that one failed proof inherently condemns an idea. Some important ideas that were initially ridiculed or rejected by experts include the following:

- The personal computer,
- The endosymbiotic theory of evolution,
- Plate tectonics and continental drift,
- Quasicrystals,
- Mendelian genetics,
- Henry Ford's assembly process,
- Georg Cantor's set theory, and
- Ludwig Boltzmann's atomic theory.

Rule # 65
Logic prohibits appeals to logic whereby something is assumed to be false simply because one proof or argument for it is invalid.

Appeals to Nature: This fallacy prohibits any argument that is based on the concept of *nature* or *natural* as inherently good and anything appearing in opposition as bad. Manufacturers and advertisers are harnessing the concept of what constitutes "nature" or the "natural" in order to capitalize on the desire of consumers to avoid the harmful additives and chemicals that make a product more profitable. With regard to food, *natural* becomes a game of characterizing ingredients versus processing. An ingredient may satisfy a definition of "natural" but may be so processed that it becomes an unhealthy ingredient. The processing of grains is but one example.

Then there is the game surrounding the label "natural." This is an advertiser's dream. For instance, if corn is grown organically, can the resulting high-fructose corn syrup be considered organic and natural? In 2008, the FDA said it may not, but this same type of question continues to play out with US consumers.

Rule # 66
Logic prohibits appeals to nature whereby whatever is "natural" or consistent with "nature" (somehow defined) is considered good, whereas whatever conflicts with nature is considered bad.

It is difficult to argue for a definitive or standardized list of logical fallacies, just as no one can claim that there is a true style of writing. Robert "Bo" Bennett is author of the book *Logically Fallacious: The Ultimate Collection of Over 300 Logical Fallacies.* From an educator's perspective, however, such an extensive list seems a bit overwhelming and, at some point, counterproductive. Some books call the same fallacy by a different name, and some lists are longer than others. This should not be seen as an academic negative, however; the fluid nature of such lists opens the door for student inquiry. Like with the seven deadly sins where debate rages over sins omitted, so, too, can the list of informal logical fallacies be debated. The Game thrives on such situations because it places the student player in the position to discover ways to add to or modify the existing list. The classroom teacher can do the same by maintaining a class list of fallacies to which students can add additional fallacies or modify the existing list.

The list-building process can be invigorated by representing the list of fallacies as not just a guiding light for good-faith thinkers but also as a proactive toolkit for those seeking to blur the line between evidence and language for the sake of profit. There is no greater tool of adolescent learning than providing students with the keys to understand how adults manipulate people for profit and power (see chapter 10).

Chapter Bibliography

Bennett, Bo. 2012. *Logically Fallacious: The Ultimate Collection of Over 300 Logical Fallacies.* Sudbury, MA: eBookIt.com.

Byrd, Robert. Robert Byrd Sums It Up, The West Virginia Senator On The Iraq War. The Progressive Review http://prorev.com/byrdtalk.html

Freud, Sigmund. (1930) 1989. *Civilization and Its Discontents.* Translated by James Strachey. London: W. W. Norton. 29 http://www2.winchester.ac.uk/edstudies/courses/level%20two%20sem%20two/Freud-Civil-Disc.pdf

Huetteman, Emmarie. November 4, 2015. "Senate Report Says Pentagon Paid Sports Leagues for Patriotic Events" New York Times, First Draft. http://www.nytimes.com/politics/first-draft/2015/11/04/senate-report-says-pentagon-paid-sports-leagues-for-patriotic-events/

Southern Education Foundation (2015) "A New Majority Research Bulletin: Low Income Students Now a Majority in the Nation's Public Schools." http://www.southerneducation.org/Our-Strategies/Research-and-Publications/New-Majority-Diverse-Majority-Report-Series/A-New-Majority-2015-Update-Low-Income-Students-Now

Steele, Bryan. 1999 *Road to Belmont.* Foreshadow Press. http://www.amazon.com/Road-To-Belmont-Bryan-Steele/dp/0970507003

CHAPTER 10

Propaganda

> If you don't want a man unhappy politically, don't give him two sides to a question to worry him; give him one. Better yet, give him none. Let him forget there is such a thing as war. If the government is inefficient, top-heavy, and tax-mad, better it be all those than that people worry over it...Give the people contests they win by remembering the words to more popular songs or the names of state capitals or how much corn Iowa grew last year. Cram them full of noncombustible data, chock them so damned full of "facts" they feel stuffed, but absolutely "brilliant" with information. Then they'll feel they're thinking, they'll get a sense of motion without moving. And they'll be happy, because facts of that sort don't change.
>
> RAY BRADBURY, *FAHRENHEIT 451*

The Game defines propaganda as "the intentional manipulation of the rules governing language." In effect, the Game's rules are subverted by the propagandist—not by accident but by intent. Instead of the rules prohibiting certain kinds of language use, the rules become part of the propagandist's proactive toolkit for manipulating audiences on behalf of those who pay.

Propaganda functions by redirecting thought away from the intellectual and toward the emotional so that members of the target audience focus on how they *feel* rather than what they might *think*, based on the evidence. From the perspective of the Game, propaganda is hazardous to human systems because propaganda inhibits the flow of accurate and timely information.

Rule # 68
All use of propaganda is prohibited.

Priming the Unconscious

Of particular importance to this discussion is the way language is harnessed as a means of manipulating the audience's unconscious. Philip Merikle from the Department of Psychology, University of Waterloo, puts it this way:

> Over the years, there have been literally hundreds of studies following a similar format. Taken together, these studies show that considerable information, capable of informing decisions and guiding actions, is perceived even when observers do not experience any awareness of perceiving.

The most direct aspect of influencing perception is the psychological concept of priming: an implicit memory effect in which exposure to one stimulus influences the response to another stimulus. Kihlstrom defines *implicit* memory as "the effect of a past event on the subject's ongoing experience, thought, and action, in the absence of, or independent of, conscious recollection of that event. Implicit memory is, in these terms, unconscious memory."

It is essential to note the fundamental difference between the way the notion of priming is understood by science, as represented above, and the way the same term is represented by the Language Manipulation Industry (LMI), which is made up of experts in communications, public relations, and advertising. The sciences of psychology and psychotherapy look at priming as a way to increase scientific understanding and help people. By sharp contrast, the LMI perceives priming as a means to exploit psychological weakness on behalf of those who pay. LMI theories that are designed to facilitate psychological exploitation include the following

- Priming theory,
- Social-learning theory,
- General-aggression model,
- Agenda-setting theory, and
- Media-influence theory.

What specifically interests the Game are the tools the LMI uses to facilitate its goals of manipulation. The discipline of logic, specifically the logical fallacies covered in the previous chapter, is designed to prohibit the manipulation of the audience's emotions.

Take any of the logical fallacies as an example of how propaganda uses these fallacies to separate language from the physical world. For example, the first logical fallacy, appeals to authority, bases an argument on the testimony of an unqualified person. If you are a public-relations expert and you need to manipulate an audience, you might consider bringing in a person who is well known and likely to influence your audience in your favor: a famous athlete or movie star, for example, even though that person is otherwise not qualified to speak authoritatively on the topic. Ask yourself, how many politicians are former athletes and movie stars? What about the Great Communicator, President Ronald Regan, or California Governor *Arnold Schwarzenegger*? While attractive and popular people can easily influence others, that attractiveness is no basis for believing their expressed opinion on topics for which they are otherwise unqualified.

Edward Bernays (1891–1995) was labeled by his *New York Times* obituary as the "Father of Public Relations" and listed as one of the one hundred most influential Americans of the twentieth century by *Life* magazine. Bernays opens his 1928 book, *Propaganda*, with the following:

> The conscious and intelligent manipulation of the organized habits and opinions of the masses is an important element in democratic society. Those who manipulate this unseen mechanism of society constitute an invisible government which is the true ruling power of our country.

Compare Bernays' view with the observations of Lord Acton thirty-three years earlier:

Power tends to corrupt, and absolute power corrupts absolutely. Great men are almost always bad men, even when they exercise influence and not authority, still more when you superadd the tendency or the certainty of corruption by authority.

Given Acton's historical observation, how did Bernays rationalize his view? The story of how Bernays became known as the Father of modern Propaganda begins with his uncle, Sigmund Freud, and an exchange of Cuban cigars for a copy of *A General Introduction to Psychoanalysis*. The BBC documentary, *The Century of the Self*, investigates the relationship between Bernays and Freud and uses interviews with primary characters, including Bernays and those who knew him. The documentary introduces Bernays with the following:

> Bernays is almost completely unknown today, but his influence on the twentieth century is nearly as great as his uncle's because Bernays was the first person to take Freud's ideas about human beings and use them to manipulate the masses. He showed American corporations, for the first time, how they could make people want things they didn't need by linking mass-produced goods to their unconscious desires. Out of this would come a new political idea of how to control the masses by satisfying people's inner selfish desires, what made them happy and thus docile. It was the start of the all-consuming self, which has come to dominate our world today. (Curtis)

Bernays' argument that humans are inherently irrational and therefore need to be controlled suffers from the fallacy of either/or, whereby there are only two options for the citizenry: being under centralized control or complete chaos. The third way would be to educate people so that they are able to self-govern their irrational impulses. Interestingly, it was Freud's daughter, Anna Freud, who followed in her father's footsteps. She became a prominent child psychologist and advocate for the importance of a socially trained ego as the antidote for human irrationality. Science took Freud's ideas one way, and business took them another.

In addition to the question of whether or not the human psyche can be influenced, notice the way Bernays advocates for structures that are explicitly prohibited by systems theory. The phrase "Those who manipulate this unseen mechanism of society constitute an invisible government" directly violates systems theory's requirement of transparency. When applied to a representative political system, there is a direct causal relationship between the ability of an electorate to hold elected officials accountable and the degree of meaningful representation provided by the system. Without transparency, there is no accountability, and without accountability, there can be no meaningful representation—placing propaganda and democracy at odds.

Some of the techniques that Bernays is credited with pioneering include the following:

- Creating the slogan "Making the world safe for democracy" for Woodrow Wilson to justify entering WWI (take a moment and ponder how this slogan is still being used today to justify war);
- Comparing "individual freedom" with the state of the individual as a collective member of society;
- Converting the term *propaganda* for use in public relations;
- Advertising cigarettes as "torches of freedom" to make smoking more attractive and socially acceptable to women;
- Creating the marketing platform "You may not need this product, but if you buy it, you will feel better";
- Creating national chains of department stores to facilitate the higher volume sales of *desired*, rather than *needed*, goods;
- Pairing his celebrity clients with his other clients' product brands in *Cosmopolitan* magazine;
- Placing his clients' products in movies;
- Using phony "independent" scientific experts and studies to sell products;
- Converting the "all-American breakfast" of coffee and toast to eggs and bacon; and
- Encouraging individuals to borrow from banks to buy stock (a pre-1929 position).

The necessary skill set for practicing propaganda is taught at our nation's best universities under the banners of public relations, advertising, and marketing. For the propagandist, language is no longer a form of responsibility to represent the physical world. Instead, language becomes a game of winners and losers in which successful language use is the product of artful spin rather than a good-faith effort to be honest.

Another propagandist of note who studied Bernays was Joseph Goebbels, Minister for Public Enlightenment and Propaganda in Nazi Germany from 1933 to 1945. Writing in his *Biography of an Idea: Memoirs of Public Relations Counsel*, Bernays comments, "Goebbels was using my book *Crystallizing Public Opinion* as a basis for his destructive campaign against the Jews of Germany. This shocked me."

Goebbels codified his studies of Freud and Bernays into his "Nineteen Principles of Propaganda" (Doob). Notice how he fashioned his ideas for a time of war. It is interesting to compare this war-ready approach with similar techniques being deployed today, not by a central government, as was appropriate during Goebbels' time, but by a new form of centralization, corporate power.

1. Propagandists must have access to intelligence concerning events and public opinion.
2. Propaganda must be planned and executed by only one authority.
    a. It must issue all the propaganda directives.
    b. It must explain propaganda directives to important officials and maintain their morale.
    c. It must oversee other agencies' activities that have propaganda consequences.
3. The propaganda consequences of an action must be considered in planning that action.
4. Propaganda must affect the enemy's policy and actions.
    a. It must suppress propagandistically desirable material that can provide the enemy with useful intelligence.
    b. It must openly disseminate propaganda whose contents or tone causes the enemy to draw the desired conclusions.

    c. It must goad the enemy into revealing vital information about itself.

    d. It must make no reference to a desired enemy activity when any reference would discredit that activity.

5. Declassified, operational information must be available to implement a propaganda campaign.

6. To be perceived, propaganda must evoke the interest of an audience and must be transmitted through an attention-getting medium.

7. Credibility alone must determine whether propaganda output should be true or false.

8. The purpose, content, and effectiveness of enemy propaganda; the strength and effects of an exposé; and the nature of current propaganda campaigns determine whether enemy propaganda should be ignored or refuted.

9. Credibility, intelligence, and the possible effects of communicating determine whether propaganda materials should be censored.

10. Material from enemy propaganda may be utilized in operations when it helps diminish that enemy's prestige or lends support to the propagandist's own objective.

11. Black, rather than white, propaganda must be employed when the latter is less credible or produces undesirable effects.

12. Propaganda may be facilitated by leaders with prestige.

13. Propaganda must be carefully timed.

    a. The communication must reach the audience ahead of competing propaganda.

    b. A propaganda campaign must begin at the optimum moment.

    c. A propaganda theme must be repeated but not beyond some point of diminishing effectiveness.

14. Propaganda must label events and people with distinctive phrases or slogans.

    a. They must evoke responses that the audience already possesses.

    b. They must be capable of being easily learned.

    c. They must be utilized again and again but only in appropriate situations.

    d. They must be boomerang proof.

15. Propaganda to the home front must prevent the raising of false hopes that could be blasted by future events.

16. Propaganda to the home front must create an optimum anxiety level.

    a. Propaganda must reinforce anxiety concerning the consequences of defeat.

    b. Propaganda must diminish anxiety (other than that concerning the consequences of defeat) that is too high and cannot be reduced by people themselves.

17. Propaganda to the home front must diminish the impact of frustration.

    a. Inevitable frustrations must be anticipated.

    b. Inevitable frustrations must be placed in perspective.

18. Propaganda must facilitate the displacement of aggression by specifying the targets of hatred.

19. Propaganda cannot immediately affect strong countertendencies; instead, it must offer some form of action or diversion, or both.

One of the best ways to bring a subject alive for students is to show them examples from history. Since the following events will be new to many students and otherwise not in their history books, it might be valuable to ask each student, as homework, to investigate one of the following or to find their own example of mixing propaganda with war.

The Vietnam War (1955–1975): In August 1964, the USS Maddox, a US destroyer on patrol in the Gulf of Tonkin, believed it had come under attack from North Vietnamese Navy torpedo boats. As such, it engaged in evasive action and returned fire. The incident led to the Gulf of Tonkin resolution, which authorized President Johnson to begin open warfare in Vietnam. It was later admitted that no attack had occurred, and in 2005, it was revealed that the National Security Agency had manipulated its information to make it look like an attack had taken place (National Security Archive).

Operation Northwoods: In 1962, the US Joint Chiefs of Staff authored a document called "Operation Northwoods," which called on the US government to stage a series of fake attacks. These proposed attacks included the shooting down of military or civilian US aircraft, the destruction of a US ship, sniper attacks on Washington D.C., and other atrocities. The idea was to blame the attacks on the Cubans as an excuse for launching an invasion. (Lemnitzer)

Persian Gulf War (1990–1991): During the Persian Gulf War, Iraq invaded Kuwait over an oil dispute. Shortly after the initial invasion, the Kuwait government hired the US public-relations firm Hill & Knowlton to influence US public opinion for about $11 million. Hill & Knowlton arranged for an appearance before a group of members of the US Congress in which a woman identifying herself as a nurse working in a Kuwait City hospital described Iraqi soldiers pulling babies out of incubators and letting them die on the floor.

Based on these accounts, the US Senate supported US military actions on behalf of Kuwait in a 52–47 vote. A year after the war, however, this allegation was revealed to be a fabrication. According to Tom Regan, writing for the *Christian Science Monitor*, the woman who had testified before Congress was found to be a member of the Kuwaiti royal family, in fact the daughter of the Kuwaiti ambassador to the US. She had not been living in Kuwait during the Iraqi invasion.

Tools of Propaganda

All of the following techniques fall somewhere within the scope of the four *D*s of propaganda:

1. Divert
2. Deflect
3. Deceive
4. Deny

Ad Nauseam: This is an argument based on repeating the point over and over again, an internal mechanism of "the Big Lie."

> "See in my line of work, you got to keep repeating things over and over and over again for the truth to sink in, to kind of catapult the propaganda."
> President George W. Bush
> Greece Athena Middle and High School
> May 24, 2005

Repeating the lie is exactly what the Bush administration did in various ways. National Security Advisor Condoleezza Rice and President Bush warned of the "mushroom cloud" that might come from Saddam Hussein's nonexistent nuclear weapons. Speaking at the Cincinnati Museum Center in 2002, Bush stated that "America must not ignore the threat gathering against us. Facing clear evidence of peril, we cannot wait for the final proof—the smoking gun—that could come in the form of a mushroom cloud."

Then there was Secretary of State Colin Powell who infamously held up fake anthrax during a presentation before the United Nations Security Council in February 2003. In these instances and hundreds like them, the Bush administration, along with corporate media outlets, catapulted its lies over and over again so that eventually the lie became truth.

Repetition is an excellent way for someone to catapult a false statement into legitimacy while making sure it stays legitimate, regardless of evidence to the contrary. The current economic notion of austerity, which requires economically struggling nations like Greece to pay off hedge fund investors first by incurring further debt and selling off state assets, such as airports and utilities, is an example of *ad nauseam*.

Economic austerity is an example of *ad nauseam* because it is assumed to be true for no other reason than because the constant claim is endlessly repeated as fact. The current use of the term *austerity* comes from a pair of respected Harvard economists Carmen Reinhart and Ken Rogoff, who was also former chief economist of the International Monetary Fund. After Reinhart and Rogoff released their 2010 paper "Growth in a Time of Debt," they went on to write a book based on the paper and followed it up by going on tour and preaching the necessity of austerity. This included an appearance before Congress. The United States, the World Bank, and the European Union, among others, all fell in line and began cutting expenditures to get out of the post-2008 crash. The strategy, however, didn't work, just as a contracting money supply had been ineffective against the onslaught of the Great Depression. As luck would have it, the banks were bailed out before anyone began any serious talk of the belt-tightening sacrifices associated with austerity. As it turned out, the work of Reinhart and Rogoff was found to be academic fraud.

Reporting for the BBC, Ruth Alexander (2013) explained how an MIT graduate student, Thomas Herndon, reran Reinhart and Rogoff's numbers. Herndon discovered that their conclusions had been based not on fact but on cherry-picked numbers they had used to get the desired result. It is hard to prove another's state of mind, but when you look at the details, there is little room in my mind for believing this was a good-faith mistake because of the following:

1. All the errors favored one outcome; and
2. The authors had already established themselves as pro-austerity.

It turns out that Reinhart and Rogoff had left out five of the twenty countries in the sample when calculating the study's key indicator, GDP growth. Herndon and his colleagues adjusted Reinhart and Rogoff's model to include the additional GDP numbers and published their results in the *Cambridge Journal of Economics*. They concluded that the correlation of debt to GDP—the underlying proof of austerity's value—was significantly less dramatic when all the numbers were included in the calculation. The spectacular results that had "proved" the value of austerity evaporated.

The belief that economic austerity is an appropriate response to the effects of bank insolvency due to irresponsible speculation exists today, in large part, because the press and academics have repeated, over and over, the idea austerity as an accepted fact ever since Reinhart and Rogoff first released their paper back in 2010.

Rule # 69
Repetition of an otherwise-unsupported idea in support of an argument is a prohibited tool of propaganda called *ad nauseam*.

The Big Lie: This expression was coined by Adolf Hitler in his 1925 autobiography *Mein Kampf*. Hitler explains

> Therewith one started out with the very correct assumption that in the size of the lie there is always contained a certain factor of credibility, since the great masses of a people may be more corrupt in the bottom of their hearts than they will be consciously and intentionally bad,

therefore with the primitive simplicity of their minds they will more easily fall victims to a great lie than to a small one, since they themselves perhaps also lie sometimes in little things, but would certainly still be too much ashamed of too great lies. Thus such an untruth will not at all enter their heads, and therefore they will be unable to believe in the possibility of the enormous impudence of the most infamous distortion in others; indeed, they may doubt and hesitate even when being enlightened, and they accept any cause at least as nevertheless being true; therefore, just for this reason some part of the most impudent lie will remain and stick; a fact which all great lying artists and societies of this world know only too well and therefore also villainously employ.

When it came time to make false statements to justify the 2003 US invasion of Iraq, President Bush said

> "In Iraq, a dictator is building and hiding weapons that could enable him to dominate the Middle East and intimidate the civilized world— and we will not allow it."
> PRESIDENT GEORGE W. BUSH, ADDRESSING
> THE AMERICAN ENTERPRISE INSTITUTE
> WASHINGTON HILTON HOTEL
> FEBRUARY 26, 2003

For a majority of US citizens, it was too much to believe a US president would make up a lie about the head of another sovereign nation in order to justify questionable military action. We are not taught about past examples of such lies in school, so we have no point of reference. Who lies about something like nuclear war? Certainly not the president of the United States.

Rule # 70
The Big Lie is a lie so "colossal" that no one would believe that someone "could have the impudence to distort the truth so infamously" is a prohibited tool of propaganda.

The Other: This is a form of appeal against the person whereby an argument casts the opposition in a negative light in contrast to the positive self-image of the speaker. This produces a kind of "us-versus-them" rhetoric. While there are numerous *others* that make up US society, there is none greater in 2016 than the Muslim. The reason a majority of US citizens believe Muslims are the nation's greatest threat is because that is what they are being told by the corporations that profit from war.

The Other: This is a form of appeal against the person whereby an argument casts the opposition in a negative light in contrast to the positive self-image of the speaker. This produces a kind of "us-versus-them" rhetoric. While there are numerous others that make up US society, there is none greater in 2016 than the Muslim. The reason a majority of US citizens believe Muslims are the nation's greatest threat is because that is what they are being told by the corporations that profit from war.

The is a rich history of creating and then using the Other as a tool of political power. President Richard Nixon used the technique of The Other to defeat both the antiwar and the black empowerment movements. John Ehrlichman was counsel and Assistant to the President for Domestic Affairs for the Nixon administration and was convicted of conspiracy, obstruction of justice and perjury. After serving his time, Ehrlichman granted an interview to author Dan Baum, wherein he recalled that

> The Nixon campaign in 1968, and the Nixon White House after that, had two enemies: the antiwar Left, and black people. You understand what I'm saying? We knew we couldn't make it illegal to be either against the war or black. But by getting the public to associate the hippies with marijuana and blacks with heroin, and then criminalizing both heavily, we could disrupt those communities. We could arrest their leaders, raid their homes, break up their meetings, and vilify them night after night on the evening news. Did we know we were lying about the drugs? Of course we did. (Baum)

The Nixon administration intentionally created a social Other to discredit its political enemies.

Rule # 71
Characterizing others as fundamentally different is a prohibited tool of propaganda called the Other.

Direct Order: This technique hopes to simplify the decision-making process by using images and words to tell the audience exactly what actions to take and eliminating any other possible choices. As authority figures can be used to give the order, it can overlap with the appeal-to-authority technique. The Uncle Sam "I Want You" image is an example of this technique.

Rule # 72
A message that dictates what is expected from an audience by eliminating the possibility of choice is a prohibited tool of propaganda called direct order.

Disinformation: Disinformation is false or inaccurate information that is deliberately spread. It is synonymous with, and is sometimes called, "black propaganda." It may include the distribution of forged documents, manuscripts, and photographs or the spread of malicious rumors and fabricated intelligence. Disinformation should not be confused with misinformation, information that is unintentionally false.

Gustave Gilbert was a medical doctor and fluent German speaker who served as a prison psychologist during the Nuremberg trials after World War II. The text of his 1947 book, *Nuremberg Diary*, is the verbatim notes Gilbert took immediately after having conversations with the prisoners. The prisoners interviewed by Gilbert included Hermann Göring, who was a leading member of the Nazi Party and designated by Hitler as his second in command. According to Gilbert, Göring made the following comment about war:

Why, of course the *people* don't want war. Why would some poor slob on a farm want to risk his life in a war when the best that he can get out of it is to come back to his farm in one piece? Naturally, the common people don't want war; that is understood.

But after all, it's the leaders of the country who determine the policy, and it's always a simple matter to drag the people along whether it's a democracy, a fascist dictatorship, or a parliament, or a communist dictatorship.

Voice or no voice, the people can always be brought to the bidding of the leaders. That is easy. All you have to do is tell them they are being attacked, and denounce the pacifists for lack of patriotism, and exposing the country to greater danger. It works the same way in any country.

One of the most shocking admonitions of intentionally lying to the public took place in a 1981 White House meeting where CIA Director William Casey reportedly said to President Richard Nixon "We'll know our disinformation program is complete when everything the American Public believes is false." (Honegger)

Rule # 73
The intentional spread of manipulated information is a prohibited tool of propaganda called disinformation.

Euphoria: This tool involves using an event that generates euphoria or happiness, or using an appealing event to boost morale. Euphoria can be created by declaring a holiday, making luxury items available, or mounting a military parade with marching bands and patriotic messages. One of the biggest public spectacles in US society today is football. As discussed in the past chapter, The Pentagon spent $53-million over 4-years to advertise war with sports leagues like the National Football League. The program was discontinued after it was exposed. Not only was it embarrassing to get caught staging euphoretic events, but the propagandistic value of euphoria significantly drops off once it is exposed as contrived.

Rule # 74
The use of public spectacle to generate emotional exhilaration is a prohibited tool of propaganda called euphoria.

Glittering Generalities: This occurs when emotionally appealing words are applied to a product or idea without any concrete argument or analysis. The greatness of service members in the US military is a common form of glittering generality used to emotionally motivate citizens to support foreign intervention. "Support the troops" is a common phrase that is an emotional concept and is not based on evidence. This glittering generality of supporting the home team distracts attention from evidence-based issues, such as the legality of attacking another country without cause, as happened during the invasion of Iraq in 2003 and Libya in 2011.

Rule # 75
Relying on emotionally appealing words for substance is a prohibited tool of propaganda called glittering generalities.

Intentional Vagueness: When arguments are made to be deliberately vague, the audience may supply its own interpretations. The intention is to move the audience by use of undefined phrases, without analyzing their validity or attempting to determine their reasonableness or application. The goal is for people to draw their own interpretations rather than for them to accept an explicit idea that is presented to them.

On September 20, 2001, a White House news release provided President Bush's explanation for why the Iraqi people are evil: because the people of Iraq "hate our freedoms—our freedom of religion, our freedom of speech, our freedom to vote and assemble and disagree with each other." (Washington Post) This notion that an entire society is driven to destroy another on the other side of the globe because they hate our freedoms is so vague that it is reasonable to assume this is an intentional use of vagueness.

A sister method to Intentional Vagueness is the use of vagueness for placing doubt in the mind of the audience. Michael Shermer, writing for *Scientific American*, uses the term *pseudoskepticism* to explain how first it was the tobacco industry that fought back against the knowledge that its consumption directly caused death. Today, Shermer points out that the same techniques are being used by the carbon industries to fight back against the fact that the burning of carbon is destabilizing the environment and causing death and destruction.

Rule # 76
Arguments that rely on deliberately vague generalities use a prohibited tool of propaganda called intentional vagueness.

Labeling: This is when the propagandist uses *euphemism* in an attempt to increase the perceived quality, credibility, or credence of a particular idea. A *dysphemism* is used when the intent of the propagandist is to discredit or diminish the perceived quality or to hurt the perceived righteousness of the mark. By creating a label, category, or faction of a population, it makes it easier for propagandists to isolate a target. For example, the radio-talk-show host Rush Limbaugh promoted the term "liberal" as a dysphemism intended to diminish the perceived credibility of liberal political positions and those who advocated them.

Rule # 77
Arguments that rely on *euphemism* to increase the value of a particular idea or *dysphemism* to decrease the value of a particular idea use a prohibited tool of propaganda called labeling.

Quotes Out of Context: This tool involves selectively editing quotes or hiding the source of a quote in order to change its meaning. One of the biggest examples of a quote that is taken out of context is the canard that US citizens have the right to bear arms. By definition, the quote is structurally out of context because it is a clause of a sentence.

The complete sentence from the Second Amendment of the Bill of Rights in the Constitution of the United States reads, "A well-regulated Militia, being necessary to the security of a free state, the right of the people to keep and bear Arms, shall not be infringed." The meaning of a sentence's clause cannot be separated from the context of the larger sentence. Hopefully one of the things students learn in high school is the nature of a sentence clause. The meaning of a sentence clause is determined by the relationship between the clause and the rest of the sentence. No sentence clause can stand on its own. Meaning is found in the entirety of a sentence not in an isolated clause. The use of an isolated clause to justify a political movement that serves the profits of gun manufactures is a classic example of using a quote out of context for the purpose of changing the meaning of the US Constitution for political and economic goals.

Rule # 78
Selectively editing quotes or hiding the source of a quote in order to change its meaning is a prohibited tool of propaganda called quoting out of context.

Rationalization: With this tool, one constructs a logical justification for a belief, decision, action, or lack thereof that was originally arrived at through a different mental process. It is a defense mechanism in which perceived-controversial behaviors or feelings are explained in a rational or logical manner in order to avoid the true explanation of the behavior or feeling in question.

Part of the rationalization for attacking Iraq was that its leader, Saddam Hussein, was a bad man. International law requires that there be cause to justify one country attaching another. That the leader of another country is "bad" is not listed as a justifiable cause. The Bush administration used the badness of Hussein as a rationalization for attack. Beyond badness not being a justification for invasion by international law, use of this justification is an excellent example of rationalization because it represents a different mental process from the ones that drive international law. The law sets specific parameters, derived by mutual agreement among signatory nations, while someone's badness is an emotional appeal that has no relation with the law.

Rule # 79
Relying on favorable generalities to justify questionable acts or beliefs is a prohibited tool of propaganda called rationalization.

Scapegoating: With scapegoating, the propagandist assigns blame to an individual or group and, thus, alleviates feelings of guilt from responsible parties or distracts attention from the need to fix the problem for which blame is being assigned. An excellent example of scapegoating is the way refugees from US wars are characterized as if they are responsible for the United States bombing their respective countries back into the Stone Age so that public institutions are ruined and civil war is allowed to rage. It is a clear disconnect of language from physical evidence to claim that the people of Iraq are better off today than when they were ruled by Saddam Hussein. Yet, it is a rare occasion to hear from the corporate media any acknowledgement that the United States is responsible for the death, displacement, and ongoing suffering of millions of Iraqi civilians as a direct result of the US embargo, invasion and occupation.

Rule # 80
Projecting responsibility for a problem onto another without cause, in order to distract attention away from the actual cause of the problem, is a prohibited tool of propaganda called scapegoating.

Slogans: A slogan is a brief, striking phrase that may include labeling and stereotyping. Although slogans may be enlisted to support reasoned ideas, in practice they tend to act only as emotional appeals. The United States is bombing other countries to "spread democracy and freedom." This slogan was first used to justify the United States entering World War I and was the phrase that vaulted Edward Bernays into his place of prominence as a propagandist. The value of this phrase is demonstrated by the fact that it is still being used a hundred years later by the same office for the same purpose. The use of this phrase is also why there is so much effort to keep alive the notion that the United States is exceptional; without it, it is hard to understand why our notion of democracy and freedom is inherently better than any other nation's notion of self-identity.

Rule # 81
Relying on brief and striking phrases (see labeling) that are emotionally appealing is a prohibited tool of propaganda called slogans.

Stereotyping: This technique attempts to arouse prejudices in an audience by labeling the object of the propaganda campaign as something the target audience fears, hates, loathes, or finds undesirable. For instance, reporting on a foreign country or social group may focus on the stereotypical traits that the reader expects even though they are far from being representative of the whole country or group; such reporting often focuses on the anecdotal. In graphic propaganda, including war posters, this might include portraying enemies with stereotypical racial features.

Serotyping can be used to create a scapegoat, as the Germans did against the Jews in World War II. The Nazi party developed a poster where a sword with a swastika stabs a snake with a Star of David on its head; the poster was labeled with the words "Usury, Versailles, Unemployment, War Guilt, Marxism, Bolshevism, Lies Deception, Inflation, Locarno, Daves-Pact, Young-Plan, Corruption, Barmat, Kutisker, Sklarek, White slavery, Terror, Civil War." Each of these terms has distinctly negative connotations that serve to stereotype a group of people in a negative light.

Nazi Anti-Semitic Propaganda Poster (ullstein bild)

Rule # 82
Relying on the arousal of prejudices in an audience by labeling the object of the propaganda campaign as something the target audience should fear, hate, loathe, or find undesirable (see labeling) is a prohibited tool of propaganda called stereotyping.

Transfer: With this tool, the propagandist passively associates *A* with *B* so that the attributes of *A* are artificially transferred onto *B*, which creates the false appearance that *A* and *B* are associated. False association through transfer is exemplified by the conflation of those who are practicing Muslims with those who seek to react to US bombing campaigns. Yes, some Muslims are so upset with having their homes destroyed and families killed by US bombs that they seek to pursue violence against anything US related. However, to say that all of the 1.5 billion Muslims in the world wish violence against others is to transfer the mind-set of a minority onto a majority: an excellent example of transfer.

Rule # 83
Redirecting blame or praise away from or toward one group or person is a prohibited tool of propaganda called transfer.

Virtue Words: These are words in the value system of the target audience that produce a positive image when attached to a person or issue. Peace, happiness, security, wise leadership, freedom, "the truth," and so on are virtue words. In countries such as the United States, religiosity is seen as a virtue.

Rule # 84
Using words in the value system of the target audience to produce a positive image when attached to a person or issue is a prohibited tool of propaganda called virtue words (see Transfer).

Complex Question: A complex question is a question that implicitly assumes something to be true by its construction, such as "Have you stopped beating your wife?" A question like this is fallacious only if the thing presumed to be true (in this case, that you beat your wife) has not been established.

Rule # 85
Relying on intentionally complex presumptions is a prohibited tool of propaganda called complex questions.

Non Sequitur (It Does Not Follow): This is the simple fallacy of stating, as a conclusion, something that does not strictly follow from the premises. For example, "Racism is wrong. Therefore, we need affirmative action." Obviously, there is at least one missing step in this argument because the wrongness of racism does not imply a need for affirmative action without some additional support (such as "Racism is common"; "Affirmative action would reduce racism"; and "There are no superior alternatives to affirmative action").

Disconnecting a conclusion from it premise(s) is problematic because it can produce faulty solutions. Affirmative action would be a nice idea if the only thing restricting the success of African Americans was the prejudice of white people. The fact is that socioeconomically disadvantaged African Americans are too often limited by substandard schools. Affirmative action often ends up compensating for substandard schools by giving a pass to those with a substandard education. The solution is to fix the schools by spending the necessary funds to compensate for economic disadvantage so that students have equal access to an education. Only once the education playing field is leveled so that everyone has a decent education can affirmative action make any sense.

Rule # 86
Relying on a conclusion that does not follow from the premises is a prohibited tool of propaganda called *non sequitur*.

Propaganda is the act of disconnecting language from physical evidence. Without language being tied to the physical world, solutions to problems will not only fall short but cause additional unintended outcomes.

Chapter Bibliography

Alexander, Ruth. 2013. "Reinhart, Rogoff, and Herndon: The Student Who Caught out the Profs." *BBC News Magazine*, April 20. http://www.bbc.com/news/magazine-22223190

Baum, Dan. 2012. The Moment: Wild, Poignant, Life-changing Stories. Edited by Larry Smith, Harper Perennial.

Bernays, Edward. (1928) 2004. *Propaganda*. New York: Ig. 37

———. 1965. *Biography of an Idea: Memoirs of Public Relations Counsel*. New York: Simon & Schuster. 128

Bush, George W. 2002. *President Bush Outlines Iraqi Threat*, October 7. Cincinnati Museum Center Cincinnati, Ohio. http://georgewbush-whitehouse. archives.gov/news/releases/2002/10/20021007-8.html

———. 2003. *President Discusses the Future of Iraq*. American Enterprise Institute. Washington Hilton Hotel. February 26, 2003. http://georgewbush-whitehouse.archives.gov/news/releases/2003/02/20030226-11.html

———. 2005. *President Participates in Social Security Conversation in New York*, Greece Athena Middle and High School. May 24. http://georgewbush-whitehouse.archives.gov/news/releases/2005/05/20050524-3.html

Curtis, Adam (director, writer). 2002. *The Century of the Self* (documentary TV series). BBC Four.

Dalberg-Acton, John (Lord Acton). 1907. "Letter to Bishop Mandell Creighton, April 5, 1887." In *Historical Essays and Studies*. Edited by J. N. Figgis and R. V. Laurence. London: Macmillan. http://history.hanover.edu/courses/excerpts/165acton.html

Doob, Leonard W. 1950. "Goebbels' Principles of Propaganda." *The Public Opinion Quarterly* 14 (3): 419–42. http://jungledrum.hopto.org/news/attachments/apr2015/goebbel_s_principles_of_propaganda.pdf

Freud, Sigmund. 1920. *A General Introduction to Psychoanalysis*. Translated by G. Stanley Hall. New York: Boni and Liveright.

———. (1930) 1989. *Civilization and Its Discontents*. Translated by James Strachey. London: W. W. Norton. http://www2.winchester.ac.uk/edstudies/courses/level%20two%20sem%20two/Freud-Civil-Disc.pdf

Gilbert, Gustave Mark. (1945) 1995. *Nuremberg Diary*. New York: Da Capo Press. 132 http://booksonline.website/book/389634.Nuremberg_Diary.html

Herndon, Thomas, Michael Ash, and Robert Pollin. 2013. "Does High Public Debt Consistently Stifle Economic Growth?: A Critique of Reinhart and Rogoff." *Cambridge Journal of Economics*. http://cje.oxfordjournals.org/content/38/2/257.full?sid=e15f3c5a-e5d4-41b9-836a-346638982e9b

Hitler, Adolf. 1941. *Mein Kampf*. New York, Reynal And Hitchcock. 313. https://archive.org/stream/meinkampf035176mbp/meinkampf035176mbp_djvu.txt

Honegger, Barbara. 1981. https://www.quora.com/Did-William-Casey-CIA-Director-really-say-Well-know-our-disinformation-program-is-complete-when-everything-the-American-public-believes-is-false?share=1 see entries by Barbara Honegger and Greg Smith

Joint Chiefs of Staff. 1962. "Operation Northwoods documents." http://nsarchive.gwu.edu/news/20010430/northwoods.pdf

Kihlstrom, John F. 1992. "The Psychological Unconscious: Found, Lost, and Regained." *The American Psychologist* 47 (6): 788–91.

Lemnitzer, L.L. March 13, 1962." Memoradum for the Secretary of Defense: Justification for US Military Intervention in Cuba" National Security Archive. http://nsarchive.gwu.edu/news/20010430/

Merikle, Philip M. 2000. "Subliminal Perception." In *Encyclopedia of Psychology*. Vol. 7. Edited by A. E. Kazdin, 497–99. New York: Oxford University Press.

National Security Archive. "The Gulf of Tonkin Incident, 40 Years Later: Flawed Intelligence and the Decision for War in Vietnam" Electronic Briefing Book No. 132. August 4, 2004. http://nsarchive.gwu.edu/NSAEBB/NSAEBB132/

Regan, Tom. 2002. *"When contemplating war, beware of babies in incubators."* *Christian Science Monitor,* September 6. http://www.csmonitor.com/2002/0906/p25s02-cogn.html

Reinhart, Carmen M., and Kenneth S. Rogoff. 2010. "Growth in a Time of Debt." Working Paper No. 15639. *National Bureau of Economic Research.* http://scholar.harvard.edu/files/rogoff/files/growth_in_time_debt_aer.pdf

Shermer, Michael. "Forging Doubt." *Scientific American,* March 2015. 74

ullstein bild. Nazi Anti-Semitic Propaganda Poster. Granger, NYC — All rights reserved.

US Constitution. amend. II.

Washington Post, The. President Bush Addresses the Nation. Thursday, Sept. 20, 2001. http://www.washingtonpost.com/wp-srv/nation/specials/attacked/transcripts/bushaddress_092001.html

CHAPTER 11

Conclusion

> And, after all, what is a lie? 'Tis but
> The truth in masquerade.
> LORD BYRON, *DON JUAN*

Writing Skills

Why does any of this matter? Because writing eighty-eight essays in four months, in conjunction with expert editing and commentary in real time by professional educators, builds thinking and writing skills in a way that is beyond the classic education model. This kind of education, where the product is the result of matching a team of professionals with daily student practice, cannot be replicated by a teacher with multiple classes each day. Most high-school educators have rosters in excess of one hundred students. These educators are responsible for creating daily lesson plans that cover multiple topics, teaching these classes, and analyzing and grading student work. There is simply not enough time to critique individual student writing day after day.

The education model described in this book takes the four responsibilities of an educator—preparation, delivery, feedback and assessment—and splits these jobs up among groups of adult professionals. The Game uses a team to prepare daily lessons in real time while otherwise managing student-initiated Game changes. Another group produces the video that delivers the lesson. The individual Gamemasters manage satellite games where they recruit players while providing players with daily feedback and assessment. In this way, the Game maintains a 30:1 player-teacher ratio so that the model is scalable without sacrificing a high quality of personal attention provided to each individual student player. The end result is the delivery of an education product that is otherwise outside the reach of the standard education model.

Raised Awareness

This form of education is also important because it raises overall awareness of the player while providing the player with an enhanced awareness of his or her environment. More information is made available to students when they are exposed to the relationship between language theory and human nature. When systems theory is added to the mix, student are equipped with the necessary tools to manage this increased body of information. The end result is students who have a greater overall awareness of themselves and the surrounding environment.

Academic Consequences

The academic consequences of a student's overall-raised sense of awareness are significant. The creation of meaningful context is the backbone of teaching; the raising of awareness is the act of creating context, which fosters learning. The Game's format creates academic context on multiple levels and, thereby, results in a higher-quality education experience.

Sociopolitical Consequences

Human systems can only hope to serve their respective mission statements when language fosters integrity between words and evidence. Rather than serve outcomes, language must serve evidence, or no new program, policy, or leader will solve our problems. It isn't even a matter of switching from capitalism to socialism if we don't first make integrity the central point of public language use.

My first paid editorial appeared in the *Los Angeles Times* the week I graduated from UC, Irvine, on June 30, 1991. This was an era that gave us the term "political correctness." I saw that this term was an attempt to put evidence-based reason on par with ideology. The political and religious forces that rely on ideology as the basis of their authority were seeing that authority eroded by evidence, and they needed a way to push back. What better tactic than to cast their evidence-based opponents as just another group of ideologues?

The problem with all this is that ideology stands still while the world changes. To rely on ideological ideas is a recipe for disaster, as change eventually catches up with stagnant thinking. Plans that are drafted and executed without a working understanding of the environment into which these plans are being deployed will, by definition, fail to achieve the intended goal. There must be integrity between language and physical evidence.

Another example of what happens when language becomes disconnected from evidence is found in the way bureaucracies function. Like political correctness, being a "team player" is another concept that supplants loyalty to the system's mission statement. Mission statements can only be served through evidence because, like nature, mission statements are indifferent to what anyone thinks and are only interested in the outcome of job performance. Yet, being a team player is too often oriented toward the political outcome of a bureaucracy rather than the bureaucracy's work product. There is no better example of this than the dysfunctional bureaucracies that run our nation's large urban school districts, as described in my book *Road to Belmont*.

The Game is also important because of the way language is manipulated to sell the policies and weapons of war. As long as our tax dollars are being used to buy weapons that are then used to kill people in other countries, no other topic can be as important. As a nation, we must stop killing foreigners for profit if we ever hope to get our domestic house in order.

We have a system where for-profit defense contractors are able to buy Congress with a small portion of the profits taken from past government contracts. These defense contractors then spread out production of each contract so that there is some form of manufacturing in each of the 435 congressional districts. This way, each US Representative will support each defense contract because a piece of each contract employs constituents. The buying of Congress and the subsequent awarding of government contracts is a self-perpetuating process. Like cancer, the corruption of our political system by the defense industry spreads to the rest of our public body. One of the few journalists follows how defense contractors influence US foreign policy is William Hartung, whose work can be found at http://www.huffingtonpost.com/william-hartung/.

To be clear, defense profits are flat during times of peace. Profit from the manufacture of bombs is only maximized if the last batch of bombs sold were used. As such, there is no way to separate increased defense profits and human blood, or as Pope Francis made the point before a group of children at the Vatican in 2015, "Some powerful people earn their living off making weapons. For this reason, many people do not want peace." The Pope went on to refer to the weapons industry as an "industry of death." What kind of society are we that so grossly disregard the Golden Rule for the sake of money?

We aren't just morally bankrupt as a nation; we behave slovenly toward our responsibilities to our own representational government as well. How else can it be explained that we are using our nation's wealth to feed a corrupt monster of defense profitability that is scorching life and property overseas while pillaging the US treasury here at home?

The US Pentagon has never been audited. How is this possible? With all the calls for accountability being directed at social programs, why isn't the same level of accountability being directed at the for-profit defense industry? Therefore, the first step in killing this beast is to remove profitability from war because profitability is the enemy of accountability. Get rid of the contractors, and you get rid of the motivation to steal US tax dollars. If we need it, if the generals say they need it, then the Pentagon builds it without any outside contractors. Whatever the military needs, it gets, just without the profit. How might such a policy impact our nuclear arsenal without General Electric's input?

With profit out of the way, you fully fund the Pentagon's office of inspector general while firing any staff with corporate ties. Then, you consolidate all the forces, so there is an army that has ships and planes and thereby eliminate the need for different branches of the government to vie for different versions of the same equipment – I say these things having served proudly as a US Marine. If these ideas were followed, I predict peace would soon follow.

Peace is more than a humanistic ideal; it directly impacts our economy and matters of social justice. As President Eisenhower said in his "Chance for Peace" speech,

> Every gun that is made, every warship launched, every rocket fired
> signifies, in the final sense, a theft from those who hunger and are not

fed, those who are cold and are not clothed. This world in arms is not spending money alone. It is spending the sweat of its laborers, the genius of its scientists, the hopes of its children. The cost of one modern heavy bomber is this: a modern brick school in more than thirty cities. It is two electric power plants, each serving a town of sixty thousand population. It is two fine, fully equipped hospitals. It is some fifty miles of concrete pavement. We pay for a single fighter plane with a half million bushels of wheat. We pay for a single destroyer with new homes that could have housed more than eight thousand people. This is not a way of life at all, in any true sense. Under the cloud of threatening war, it is humanity hanging from a cross of iron…Is there no other way the world may live?

As university humanities departments continue to shrink while departments of communication grow, our use of language has become so corrupt that we are losing our ability to understand ourselves and the greater world. We have moved to a cultural understanding of language that is so disconnected from physical evidence that to even suggest any form of accountability is met with derision and charges of political correctness.

As our relationship with physical evidence goes, so goes our public institutions, where mission statements are made irrelevant without the inclusion of relevant evidence for the purpose of accountability. The result is bureaucracies that become fat and lazy, indifferent to any information except for how something might influence private sector profit and internal politics.

Language has become commodified so that loyalty is not to evidence but to profit. I don't think it is a coincidence that the commodification of language follows the same trajectory as the beginning of moving labor offshore in the mid-1970s and the dramatic shift in tax liabilities for corporations and wealthy individuals, where a large chunk of the nation's tax burden was shifted from the wealthy to the nonwealthy. The end result is bureaucracies that became more dysfunctional as tax bases dropped, resulting in budgets getting squeezed amid internal dysfunction.

This breakdown is an outcome that seamlessly fulfills the dreams of the neoliberal agenda. The poster child for the movement, Grover Norquist, commented in an NPR interview that "I'm not in favor of abolishing the government. I just want to shrink it down to the size where we can drown it in the bathtub." Norquist is also the author and advocate of an antitax pledge his group requires of Congress members if they wish to receive corporate money and thereby remain in office. It is through the lowering of taxes that the military side of government starves nonmilitary spending programs that began under the FDR administration.

As stated at the beginning of this book, the individual ideas discussed here are not new. A great deal of the larger argument is captured by Barry Levinson, the Academy Award-winning director, screenwriter, and producer. Writing for *The Huffington Post* in 2013, Levinson provided the following satirical interview with the fictitious Dr. R. H. Flutes, who heads up the Lying Institute of America. Flutes' Institute, we are told, "has schooled hundreds of politicians both on the local and the national level to help them refine their lying skills."

Q: How do you evaluate the political lying these days?

Dr. R. H. Flutes: Well, lying has entered a new phase.

Q: I don't understand, are you saying lying is evolving?

Dr. R. H. Flutes: Well, the new age tactic is to devalue the English language. It's more sophisticated.

Q: Can you be more specific?

Dr. R. H. Flutes: Well, an example: Grover Norquist, who was the forerunner of devalued English, continues to lead the charge in the twenty-first century. He continues to say his goal is to shrink government and then drown it in the bathtub. But what he is really saying is I want a revolution, I want to overturn this democracy and create a new government.

Q: Isn't he just using that term as a metaphor?

Dr. R. H. Flutes: What is the metaphor? He said he wants to kill the government in a bathtub. The only substitute is overturn the government.

He is a revolutionary like Lenin or Mao. He doesn't believe in the system. He just doesn't want to say it with as much clarity as they did.

Q: What's the reason for that?

Dr. R. H. Flutes: Because you can't get on talk shows if you're a self-proclaimed revolutionary. You have to devalue the language. Make what you say confusing. Because sometimes people think that confusing language is a sign of intelligence.

Q: But Doctor, he just wants to lower taxes.

Dr. R. H. Flutes: If you just want to lower taxes, is it necessary to drown the government in a bathtub? Simply say you want a lower tax code. Period. Drown the tax code, if you will. But he wants to drown the government of the United States. Kill what the founding fathers fought for.

Q: Don't you think you're over stating his goals?

Dr. R. H. Flutes: No. He states his goals in devalued English. That way he remains respectable. Let me ask you a question: Norquist says he is trying to change the tone in the state capitals and turn them toward bitterness and partisanship. How do you interpret that? I'll tell you. He doesn't believe in a democracy because it's obvious that he does not believe in an exchange of ideas. A democracy is based on the power of the people. He doesn't believe in the people. What he is saying in using devalued English is I want absolute power and I have contempt for those who don't agree. He uses the idea of state legislators as the shield for what he really wants. He wants power, control. Devalue the language, my friend. Make it murky. Remove clarity. Get attention. It's the new form of lying.

Q: But he is respected for the most part.

Dr. R. H. Flutes: Here is another quote from him: "Bipartisanship is another name for date rape." Actually, he took that from Dick Armey.

Q: Well that doesn't make any sense.

Dr. R. H. Flutes: No kidding. But it is a flavorable use of words. Let me put it to you another way—let's say his name is not Grover Norquist. He is a black man, or a Latino, or for that matter any minority and he says (as Norquist did), "Our goal is to inflict pain. It is not enough to win. It has to be a painful, devastating defeat. Like when the king would take his opponents head and spike it on a pole for everyone to see." If you were any of those minorities, they would lock you up and throw away the key. Devalued language requires white respectability.

Q: All these vitriolic statements because he is opposed to taxes?

Dr. R. H. Flutes: No, you keep missing the point. It is not only about taxes. He is opposed to this government. The US government. He is a new kind of revolutionary. A twenty-first-century revolutionary.

Q: And he didn't attend the Lying Institute of America?

Dr. R. H. Flutes: No, he was tutored by a great nephew of P. T. Barnum.

A healthy society cannot coexist with language that is devalued and in service to an unrelated agenda. We are losing our freedom of self-determination because academia and the greater society have allowed language to become a disconnected hustle rather than a personal and social responsibility. It is time to change the way we teach high-school English, or we will continue to devolve into a neo-feudal society that asserts dominant control, as the Catholic Church once did, through the control of language.

Chapter Bibliography

Pope Francis. n. d. "Pope Francis to children: Peace is a craft built every day with love." Translated by Rome Reports in English. https://www.youtube.com/watch?v=JWbeh44pBbA&feature=youtu.be

Dwight D. Eisenhower. 1953. "The Chance for Peace." Speech to the American Society of Newspaper Editors, April 16. http://www.presidency.ucsb.edu/ws/index.php?pid=9819

Levinson, Barry. 2013. Grover and the Bathtub. The Huffington Post. March 14, 2013 http://www.huffingtonpost.com/barry-levinson/grover-and-the-bathtub_b_2879088.html

Norquist, Grover. 2001. *Morning Edition.* National Public Radio, May 25, 2001. http://www.npr.org/templates/story/story.php?storyId=1123439

CPSIA information can be obtained
at www.ICGtesting.com
Printed in the USA
LVOW02s1127180216

475646LV00013B/74/P